T0196033

Navigating
The Winds of Change

A Spiritual Guide To Embracing A Loving Life

Steven Mana Trink

BALBOA.PRESS
A DIVISION OF HAY HOUSE

Balboa Press books may be ordered through booksellers or by contacting:

Balboa Press
A Division of Hay House
1663 Liberty Drive
Bloomington, IN 47403
www.balboapress.com
844-682-1282

Cover Design and Art by Steven Mana Trink

Print information available on the last page.

ISBN: 978-1-9822-5206-9 (sc)
ISBN: 978-1-9822-5208-3 (hc)
ISBN: 978-1-9822-5207-6 (e)

Library of Congress Control Number: 2020914054

Balboa Press rev. date: 12/11/2020

Contents

Dedication

I dedicate this book in loving memory
of my beautiful, compassionate, humble,
aloha spirited wife and soul partner
Dr. Laura Bella Moire.

Dr. Laura was devoted to helping and supporting the underdogs and the less fortunate. She was always freely providing her services to those who were in need of medical care or were being faced with life threatening circumstances. Her "Light" continues to reside in the hearts of all the lives she touched. Laura Bella, the name she loved to answer to, was born the very Saint that she as a child always dreamed of growing up to become.

Foreword

I met Steven Mana Trink, many years ago and was immediately impressed with his desire to help people evolve spiritually and consciously. In addition to his being a Master Hypnotist and experienced in the field of Epigenetics, Mana is a natural mentor. His eagerness to bring out the best in every situation and in everyone is heartfelt. Beyond that, the level of creativity that has flowed in the last years, in both his artistic and written expression—is truly extraordinary. It seems to defy logical explanation, and one cannot help but ask: Where did it come from?

A few years ago, Mana experienced an intense personal challenge when he had an accident causing severe injuries to his body coupled by the death of his life partner Laura. The tragic events propelled him into a higher vibrational understanding of "What Is." His book reveals how our life's experiences along with its' greatest hardships can compel us to go deeper into our heart - consciousness, a place of infinite insights and discoveries.

I have been on the path of self-realization ever since I was introduced to metaphysics in 1971. I had experienced deep depression on and off throughout my 20's trying to heal what I perceived as a separation from God. I was able to overcome the depression, but my quest for spiritual growth never ended. Since then I have dedicated my life to teaching and building community, including the founding of the "Sacred Friends Community" in order to introduce spiritual teachers and concepts to a broad swath of people, now numbering in the thousands. (I have been affectionately dubbed "The Goodwill Ambassador for the Southern California Conscious Community."

Due to my keen interest in metaphysics and spiritual consciousness for more than four decades, I have had the opportunity to read countless numbers of books on these subjects. Mana's book stands out among them. He takes us on a deep dive into the void that exists beyond the limitations of the mind and powers us into an understanding of the immense clarity that can come when we surrender to the infinite wisdom of our inner internal home, a fertile place perfectly aligned with the principals that guide our Universe and its Divine Knowingness. Many other authors have tackled that subject before, but Steven Mana Trink pays special attention to the importance of embracing the sacred wisdom of the heart.

At the Source of *"All That Is"* resides a guidance that is always at our side helping us grow on all levels, even if we resist. At its core, that guidance longs to take us to the next level of expansion and development for our highest good. Often all we need to do is get out of our own way and simply surrender. But how does one go about this?

Mana points out the vital importance of being able to view the ego-minds' agenda, while simultaneously putting one's attention on taking a deep dive into the immensity and wonderment of the wisdom of the heart. After pointing out all the ways of how the ego is our driving force, he shows us that we are left with the only real choice; to submit to the passion that resides in the heart.

Ultimately, by developing our compassionate nature, we are able to be a divine steward to that which is most high, the inner calling, the *I Am That I Am,* that rests at the root of the captivating unfolding journey of one's life.

This book offers an opportunity to experience and tap into your inner wisdom from many diverse angles so that you can come to know the illusive zone that often seems impenetrable. You are encouraged to take this leap of faith across the precipice into the "Limitless Unknown" where, ironically, as it turns out, is where all possibilities and miracles reside.

When you read "Navigating The Winds of Change" you will be invited to become a servant to your all-knowing compassionate heart.

This all-embracing book definitely changes your awareness in your quest for enlightenment. It provides a rare entry into the "quickening" of the divine process. "Navigating The Winds of Change" is full of insights, love, and empathy for the human condition that will uplift your mind and open your heart to new levels of understanding, compassion, and unconditional love for yourself and all of humanity. You will find that the sharing of Mana's experiences and insights is both elevating and inspiring. Enjoy the journey...

Samuel Kiwasz, "Goodwill Ambassador for the Southern California Conscious Community"

I was told in the quietude of my space that I have been blessed with knowledge prior to coming to this reality. Supported and guided, I experienced the linear world, which provided the lens of duality that is required for perception of the absolute.

"All is as it has always been" was a theme that needed to be heard throughout my journey in the land of Now. Spirit reminded me of the purpose of this time around. I was empowered by the energy of its truth.

Introduction

It is my heartfelt vision that this book ignites, inspires, and motivates all who are being called to the possibilities and miracles that wait in both grace and trust for us to experience fully our humanness. This is the path that we are asked to follow in this lifetime, when our consciousness is at its highest crest in the evolution of humankind.

When we accept and embody our divine selves in every moment, we get to be the director of the story of our lives. As we journey toward self-mastery, we become aware that the highest expression of our divine essence is in the knowing that all of it is our own creation. The guidance I am presenting harnesses our fullest potential from the position of heart-centered inner strength, rather than from a position of might. I share with you the wisdoms, insights, truths, and knowledge that have been revealed to me along my path in humanity's journey of enlightenment.

The stories that were woven by the ego's hidden agenda to separate us from our inheritance had deprived me many times from experiencing the joy and the celebration of my life. However, they set the stage for what was yet to come. The experiences I encountered were divine lessons that would point me toward a way to liberate myself from my ego-mind's projected fears and illusions. Spirit became my guide. I was being led to welcome another reality, and the challenges proved to be opportunities for my spiritual growth.

Prior to my awareness of spirituality, I was absent from the knowledge that I had a choice between identifying with the illusions of my mind-made reality and embracing the truth that resides in the heart. The ego wanted to define my identity. It wanted to own me. Its intention was to link my very existence to the linear and logical dialogue of the mind. Its mission was to hide the truth that lies in the consciousness of the heart. I was consistently striving to free myself from an existence filled with drama, conflicts, and emotional pain. After experiencing many recurring life lessons, I came to understand how the universe works and the part I play in the grand symphony of life. As I surrendered to the consciousness of the heart, allowing it to illuminate my path and guide me with its wisdom, I discovered the secret my ego had kept hidden in the fear of its' death: *I am love.*

I have now realized that true evolution of consciousness arises from the vulnerability of an open heart and from the trust in the divinity of the process—embracing the embodiment of love is the souls yearning purpose. What also became very clear to me is how the ego-mind pretends to be your friend. It creates the illusion of living in a predicable world where we have assumed control over our outcomes, so we can feel progressively safe and secure in our decisions. In essence, by its innate nature, the ego-mind defends itself against the very transformation that liberates us from the struggle of desperately needing and striving.

The chapters are divided into segments of twenty-one days and are best individually studied with the intention of integrating the insights, truths, and wisdoms into our daily life. Instead of simply intellectualizing or conceptualizing, we change the way in how we experience our individual reality when embodying and living the wisdom. In this way, we become the masters of our own destiny; the unfolding adventure takes place on its own as our reality encompasses a grander perception This awareness comes from being in Oneness with the creative consciousness of love and therefore liberated from the trappings of the ego-mind.

I took the liberty to honor the sacredness that certain words represent by capitalizing the first letter. Throughout the book, I emphasize bringing your attention to specific buzzwords and phrases by using italics. If there are words that you are unsure as to their spiritual meaning, please refer to the spiritual glossary for a more detailed explanation.

The best approach to putting the information that is presented to you into a format that you can apply in your daily life is to treat it as if you were attempting to put a picture jigsaw puzzle together, piece by piece. Allow the heart to explore your findings. Stay open for transformation. Eventually, it all comes into place, and you will have an *oh-wow* moment, which I have always viewed as a holy moment—a blessing.

I invite you to visit my website *stevenmanatrink.com* and download your Bonus copy of the workbook "Perceptions". This insightful, artistic and vibrantly activating adjunct to *Navigating The Winds of Change* presents the opportunity for you to embark on a journey of discovery that opens the door to a new reality and the embracement of your true nature.

The *intentions* that are found in the "Reflections" at the end of each chapter are designed to plant your subconscious mind with seeds of love. Read them twice daily, preferably in the morning upon awakening and at night just prior to going to sleep.

By the fact that you are being guided to read these words and are drawn to explore the path that leads to the infinite destination of your eternal journey is confirmation that you are bathing in the river of miracles.

You have begun to explore the possibilities of self-expression as you focus your perception on the unity and Oneness that encompasses all creation. You have chosen the human form as a way to express your divine essence and embrace your true identity: love.

I am truly thrilled to take this journey with you.

Day One

The Winds of Change

Our lives as we once knew them are radically changing. It is time to awaken to the integral part we play in the transformational journey we have chosen to take in the advancement of Humankind. We are on the crest of an evolutionary shift in consciousness—a higher level of awareness where life takes on a new perspective.

To be born in these times, in the evolution and on the crest of a spiritual awakening, is a gift and an opportunity that our souls have presented to us. We are here to experience the blessing in the human vessel that houses our spirit and life force expressing our souls purpose. We have also chosen this time in our journeys to partake in a global shift of consciousness that encompasses a higher octave of perception that reflects all of creation and in doing so embraces love as the only reality.

Being part of the universal creation, we are always in a kinetic state of evolving. We just have to observe nature for its validation as it unfolds in the most divine and sacred way in the perfection of infinite change.

The wind is a wonderful metaphor to symbolize this creative force, as is all of nature. Along with change comes the human mind's intervention, wanting to know what the wind will bring, for our minds seek comfort in knowing what is going to happen next—to control the outcome so we can be safe and secure. We have been conditioned and programmed to believe that we can gain control over the natural state of our experiences based on this perceived illusion.

Life is a dance of transit, impermanence, and the experience of the reality of now. It gives us the absolute opportunity to express our divine essence and offers the blessing of enlightenment. Therefore, by surrendering to the will of the wind we are carried to the heights of the experience of being alive and to the ultimate expression of our divine selves.

> *The vehicle on the path of enlightenment is change.*
> *It is an ongoing journey absent of an ending,*
> *always unfolding into the eternity of love.*

Although my story along this road of perpetual enlightenment is different than yours, we still walk on the same path toward a shared destination that will always remain our home. Our separate life adventures have brought us to an extraordinary crossroad. All that is required in this moment is our surrender to the divinity of a new reality. This is what waits for us. It will require our full participation and the awareness of self as we reach out, open the door, and step over the threshold to experience, embody and celebrate the consciousness of love.

The path of spiritual enlightenment we have chosen to follow is a solo voyage. It is about blindly taking each step in our unfolding story, as we must trust in the divinity of the process. The journey is about self-empowerment and our acceptance of our divine selves. We are shown the way simply by listening to our own inner guidance— the voice from within that emanates from our hearts, unencumbered by the thinking mind, in the unfolding stories of our lives. It will always lead us into the light.

Now that I am at this juncture in my experiences of life, there is only moving forward, consciously devoted to continuing on my sacred journey to the eternal destination we are all seeking: the reality beyond the concept of life and death, ultimately revealing the Oneness that always has been present.

As we stand on the very edge of our gravest fear—uncertainty—we have the choice to take a leap in faith into a higher consciousness, a place where our ego-minds have always feared to tread. We are being asked to relinquish, detach, and release all attachment to outcome and results, and to live in the hands of trust. It took courage to follow the call of the heart in order to get to this step, and it takes devotion to open the door, cross over the threshold, and experience just how high we can soar.

As we spread our wings and ride the winds of change, we ascend beyond the mind's imagination. The currents, sometimes turbulent, always provide the necessary uplift to guide us to our destinations: the celebration of the liberation of our spirits and discovery of the divinity within ourselves.

I value all my experiences, specifically the ones that have been painful, for they brought me to this very sacred moment in my spiritual growth and the remembering of my divine connection.

> *Enlightenment is discovering what we already are.*

If I changed even one thought, decision, choice, or action along the way, everything from that point on would affect the reality that I perceive to be my life now. In my discovery that life itself is the consciousness of Oneness, I truly love that I am that. Love and consciousness are one and the same.

Our journeys are infinite. We can expect our lives to come around full circle in the course of this voyage. It is a continuous succession of experiences that allows us to observe our own reflections in every scenario. The perception of our realities has been coauthored and gifted by the universe. We scripted our stories in order to discover our wisdom, celebrate our divinity, and embrace the physicality of love. The very heart of the journey is to be at our highest potential and at our fullest expression in our human bodies. This means the embodiment of Oneness—the loving consciousness that flows through all of creation and resides in the depths of our inner beings.

Know that the truth we seek is within all of us. When we make the transition from *believing* to *Being,* we are in the process of embodying the Oneness with all of life. We get to taste the experience of divine connection and bathe in the sacred waters of our core essence. It is a path that must be traveled alone if it is to lead to the destination that we have come here to remember. It is a journey of the heart and a focus of intent to be in unity with the frequencies of divine love. Our trust and devotion is needed in order to be totally present in our journeys and allow for the highest choices to be made so that our divine essence is expressed to its fullest.

I have been asked over the years to write a book and to impart the wisdom that I have been blessed with. It is in my joy that I gladly share with you my experiences, knowledge, discoveries, teachings, and insights that I have encountered in my journey of enlightenment in trust that we will transcend the limitations of the human mind by experiencing, embracing, and celebrating our own divinity—the essence of who we really are.

> *Being transcends the need for belief.*

Reflections

Inspirations Ignited by the Soul

*"I choose to shift my awareness to the truth that has
been revealed within the depths of my own heart."*

The truth that arises from the Heart is the essence of purity and completeness. It carries the reality of love and the organic beginning of creation. It is the only truth that exists. It is the truth that will always remain the same. It is eternal, forever and always.

All that lies outside the truth is the illusion
and therefore truth is our only reality.

Give yourself permission to allow your mind to focus on what is beautiful and loving in your life. In this vision you find what it is you have always been searching for. Holding this awareness calls forth the birthing of more Joy, Harmony and Love until it becomes embodied by your experience of complete bliss.

Claim your *Bonus Gift* of the workbook "Perceptions" that compliments *Navigating The Winds of Change*. It is available as a *free* download on my website. The high frequency and vibrant artwork activates your feelings of harmony, peace and joy. Take the opportunity to continue on a journey of discovery expanding your perception, awareness and embracement of your core essence: Love

Day Two

The Calling

The manifestation of events that change brings becomes our physical reality. They are divine plays in consciousness and the unfolding creative expression of the universe. The process is one that introduces us into a new level of perception, embracement, and celebration of reality—one that effortlessly propels itself on the currents of life.

During the course of my youthful years, I was fixated on the material perspective of living a successful life. Of course, my definition of success was different than what I have grown to value now. I focused on making money; building successful businesses; growing a family; getting a divorce from Sandy, my first wife; and moving to California from Brooklyn, New York. They were busy and stress-filled years, all in preparation for what was yet for me to experience in my journey along the path of enlightenment.

My children from my fist marriage, Brian and Erica, were young at the time when I was inspired to follow an opportunity that would forever change the direction of my life as I knew it to be. It was a call from the universe that rang loud—a very clear and gentle voice within. I was being guided. I was very secretive in sharing my thoughts with my family or friends in fear of any resistance, based on their linear logic and reasoning.

I began by relinquishing my ownership of a national sales organization in the apparel industry that I had founded with my business partner, proceeded to initiate a separation with my first wife after ten years of marriage, packed one bag, closed my eyes, and, in a blind leap of faith, boarded a plane headed to Los Angles, California.

I felt like I was taken by a storm: the winds of change had dropped me into never-never land, the ultimate land of fantasy. I believed the illusion that I was free of my past. I was having a grand time. I looked at my move to the West Coast as the ticket to my freedom from a life of striving.

Following 1976, the year I landed in Southern California, I continued in a career of merchandising, designing, sales, and manufacturing of apparel. I identified myself through my ego-mind's perspective and resumed to live in a world where my consciousness was tied to the illusionary stories of my mind-made reality. I had zero idea of what was yet to manifest for me and how my life would unfold into what I now experience as the celebration.

On a cloudy, misty day in October, I found myself sitting on the beach in Marina del Rey, California, depressed and confused, alone in my thoughts. "What is wrong with this picture?" came a voice from within. I finally opened my eyes to the reality that even though I moved to a new environment; I took my old self with me. If my life was to change, then the change must come from within.

In the time to come, I ventured into a new marriage with Christel, who showed up in my story as a guiding light. She blessed me with a second daughter, Tassia, who became an ER nurse and resides in Long Beach, California. I went on to live in Marina del Rey, Dana Point, and Malibu—all magnificent settings located along beautiful landscapes and pristine beaches. I adventured to many wonderful and exciting destinations outside this country, skied in the mountains of Mammoth, and enjoyed the beach and surf of the California coast.

When we are in the storm, all we see is the clouds. When we focus above the clouds, the blue sky and the brilliance of the sun are visible. It is and always will be all perfect and in divine order. Our life experiences are reflective of nature providing us with either bright or dreary days where our skies are filled with sunshine or dark clouds. How else could we learn to navigate through the storms except through our experiences? The beautiful thing is that once we become conscious of the lesson the experience brings and integrate the wisdom gleaned from the encounters in our lives, there is zero need to attract that particular lesson again.

The silence that remains after the roar of the ego,
The essence of truth still centered in the heart,
My spirit guides me through the storm,
I feel the trust
I experience the dawn.

It was in 1996 that Christel and I took separate paths; however, we always remain friends in support of each other and our daughter. It was a time when I began to appreciate my journey—one that brought me to the doorstep of a spiritual adventure and into a realm of a higher awareness, accessing the ancient wisdom that always silently resided within me.

My experiences started to take on another perspective when I was first introduced to hypnosis as a way to remove limiting blocks that held me back from detaching from my conditioned belief system. I was devoted and open to trying many different avenues and modalities over the following years in order to move past my mind's agenda of tethering me to a false identity, depriving me of my inheritance of joy and the embracement of self love.

The key reason I was first drawn to hypnosis, a powerful modality that addresses the subconscious mind and the part of the brain that stores all our beliefs and memories as a known truth, was that hypnosis was my last resort. After going to psychologists, psychiatrists, group therapies, and workshops, I was better able to understand, conceptualize, and intellectualize some of the dynamics and experiences that led to my challenges, but very little really changed for me. I continually kept searching for joy and love.

In my search for other holistic, alternative ways, I was guided to exploring hypnosis and energy healing, both of which contributed to my opening up of new pathways to a higher consciousness and awareness, raising the curtain, and lifting the veil to love's presence.

I enrolled in courses and studied with masters. I began to see life through a new set of lenses, rejecting the illusions and embracing truths. Life began to take on a new meaning. The light of spirit, which was channeled into my subconscious mind through hypnosis, was the road to healing. My experiences eventually led me to become a clinical master hypnotherapist, helping others to open the door and cross over the threshold into a new reality. I embraced my new path and the feeling of gratitude—the ultimate state of receivership—for the passion that was revealed. I knew that my contribution to this planet would be in sharing my discoveries and shining my light on all those who are seeking liberation from the darkness.

My knowledge of the many tools and processes that were used in the healing arts arena expanded as I opened myself up to the adventure, devouring what I was learning and embracing the possibilities. I was dancing between two worlds—the world I was born into (one of stories, illusions, and mind-made realities) and the world of miracles, possibilities, and experiences that lies beyond the mind's storytelling. Having one foot in each world made it difficult to be in alignment with my integrity. I was being shown another way. I chose to surrender the struggle and follow what it was that my heart was leading me to. I closed the door on the past and fully stepped into the world of healing. I created a private practice guiding individuals who were ready to accept a new reality. My training and experience over the past twenty-five years in hypnosis, epigenetics, energy healing, and vibrational medicine woven with my spiritual journey brought about wonderful changes and miraculous healings in myself and other people's lives. I was experiencing a magnificent sense of fulfillment. *I found my calling.*

During the time I had my practice located in Marina del Rey, I met Cecilia, who divinely walked into my office and consequently into my life. She was a young Brazilian woman with a radiant character that freely expressed love and vibrancy. She navigated solely through the guidance of her higher self.

Our scripts were written long ago. It is obvious to me today that her presence in my life was to guide me in my journey to this very moment. We started our relationship in a conventional way; however, one day after waking up and having breakfast together, our relationship unexpectedly changed. I was sitting across from my spirit guide in disguise and a threat to my ego's very existence. She appeared from the ethers and sprinkled angel dust on all that she touched. The house we lived in together was sacred and magical. It was a place for transformation, a beautiful home that became our sanctuary and my monastery, situated on a mountaintop, above the clouds, overlooking the Pacific Ocean, Malibu, and Chumash Indian ceremonial grounds. It was a mystical time surrounded in the reality of truth and wisdom. After four years of teachings and shining her guiding light upon me Cecilia's own journey eventually led her to adventure into the jungles of Hana, Hawaii. I was now set free to soar on my own—to see how high I could fly. Today, Cecilia still remains one of my closest friends and my greatest teacher.

In 2005, at the age of sixty-three, after returning from a spiritual quest in Peru, my focus intensified and continued to be about embracing the spirit of life. I divinely met Laura who literally showed up at my doorstep in Malibu soon after I returned back from my life-shifting adventure. The universe was making a home delivery. Laura was my first initiation into a world filled with the Aloha spirit. Our hearts united before the mind even became aware of the union. We were blessed with the opportunity to be able to express our true selves in the complete acceptance of each other's love.

I can truly say that throughout all my relationships over the years and with the knowledge that life gives us an opportunity to express our divine essence and embody our fullest potential, I was able to experience the purity of love, free of need for the first time. It was our souls' greatest gift to each other.

Our paths were in harmony as we supported our partnership with acceptance, trust, compassion, and love. I was zero prepared or even expectant of Laura to show up in my story. However, the universe always dances in synchronicity, and her presence was in perfect timing.

During one of my many visits to Oahu with Laura, we visited a sacred Hawaiian ceremonial site on top of a mountain on the North Shore. I soon discovered that I was in the presence of a medicine woman who had provided medical care to the Kahunas, an elder generation of Hawaiian shamans and medicine men. She was trusted and welcomed as their equal. They honored her by sharing their secrets and healing modalities.

When we reached the top of the ceremonial grounds, we came to view a large hut the Hawaiians named the Mana Hale, interpreted as the House of Mana. It was the sacred place where all weapons were stored during the Hawaiian worship of the Pleiadian star system. Dr. Laura, the medicine woman, then gifted me with the name Mana, which has the meaning in the Hawaiian language of "power, source, or divine energy." Ever since then, I have grown into and embraced *Mana* as my spiritual name.

Laura's brilliance and passion for being of service is credentialed by her experiences in the past thirty years as a board-certified ER physician. She was also board-certified in integrative world medicine, a new specialty that treats the whole person instead of just the symptom. While still a resident of the Big Island for twenty-seven years, she enjoyed working on Indian reservations and in rural areas across the mainland where she could practice *true* medicine instead of merely processing patients.

She always talked about taking a leap in faith by leaving the medical arena, which had changed so dramatically over the years, to follow her heart. I was totally enrolled in supporting her vision. In June 2015, after two years of envisioning and designing for what was to become Priority Care Hawaii, a 24/7 hotel/house call medical urgent care service, we moved permanently from one paradise in Malibu, California, to another, the Waikoloa Beach Resort area on Hawaii's Big Island. Laura was going to be able to practice medicine from her heart, the way medicine used to be: zero insurance and pharmaceutical companies dictating health care or profit-minded hospital administrators.

By the middle of November, the beginning of the holiday season, we were ready to provide medicines and urgent medical care to the bedside of visitors and travelers who were staying in the many hotels, resorts, and vacation rentals along the Kona Coast. It was a service that was deeply appreciated and embraced by the community from the moment we made our first house call.

All my years of life experiences provided me with perspective. Looking back, I could then see that the riding of the merry-go-round, trying to catch the brass ring, and harnessing the illusion of success were tainted by my conditioned values and my destructive ego-mind. For the first time ever, I felt the blessing of being totally fulfilled. My value of success had shifted. It was now related to the degree of how much I embraced, embodied, celebrated, and shared, in loving Oneness, my true self in the beautiful experiences encountered in the harmony of joy.

It really takes very little effort to experience the richness of life if we come from the place of allowing rather than trying to control life out of fear. The resistance I was initially faced with was in truly giving myself permission to be open to receive the gifts that the universe was presenting and eventually trusting the divine process.

We must be certain about what we truly wish to experience and embody as the heart's desire. Clear intent is necessary so that we are broadcasting to the universe at a frequency that will attract into our lives the loving choices we make in our journeys. Our lives have now become about the awareness of energies as we vibrationally align to a heart-centered consciousness

Living in the paradise of Hawaii, empowered by a loving consciousness while holding the space for transformation and healing, brought forth a deep gratitude, appreciation and declaration of all that I was experiencing.

In September 2016, we came upon a fork in the road. Laura was diagnosed with cancer of the cervix. Her surgery was deemed successful. A year later the disease came back as fourth-stage clear-cell carcinoma, a rare and aggressive cancer. Laura's options were minimal, so she sought treatment outside the country. I became her caretaker as she wrestled with her challenge. The winds of change took us both on another path.

Reflections

Inspirations Ignited by the Soul

*"I am discovering within myself a level of
perception that is both new and beautiful"*

The experiences we have along our path of self- discovery are
based on the perception or viewpoint of the one who is having the
experience and always reflect our choices. We can choose to follow
the illusionary stories the ego- mind creates or choose to come from
a place that is heart- minded and view life through the eyes of Love
and experience the Beauty in all of Creation. It is your birthright to
live in the "Light".

Was there a time in your journey where your intuitive inner guidance
was leading you in a direction that was contrary to the reasons of the
logical mind and defied what others may have advised?

Imagine how your life would be now if you continually took a leap of
faith into the void of the infinite and choose to trust and embrace the
possibilities, miracles and the richness of life with each encounter.

Day Three

Infinite Possibilities

In the continuing unfolding scenario of the story of my life that I co-created for myself, I had fallen, shattered my shoulder, and fractured my pelvis. The scene took place on a dark and rainy night in the handicapped parking lot of the hospital where I had just brought Laura to be admitted on an emergency basis. Her diagnosis was grave. Later that evening, it was agreed that I should go back home, freshen up, get some rest, and come back in the morning. However, the universe had different plans. The following morning, I awakened to find myself in the hospital room across from Laura in pain, unable to walk or use my right arm. The accident confined me to a rehabilitation facility for five weeks that kept me from physically being with her in the time she needed me the most.

Instead of making me a victim, the incident elevated me to a higher consciousness in my soul's journey, which I was able to realize as I looked back on the pure essence of the experience. The wisdoms and insights that were embraced are priceless gifts to embody and share.

The circumstances we attract in our lives give us the opportunity to be in the present moment. It is in this moment we can make choices from the perspective of heart-centeredness, and reveal our true identities, our divine essence, which always remains the same in light of any life-changing events that we are presented with.

The final scene in Laura's life came to a closing in March 2018. The experience brought me to a new level of awareness with the intimacy of love and my relationship with death. Change provides and opens the door to a higher level of vibrational energy that supports navigating in trust through the experiences of life.

A few days after her passing, I developed a pulmonary embolism, which is a blood clot in the lungs, and was flown to a hospital on the island of Oahu, unable to attend Laura's end-of-life celebration. It was more than two years before I was able to return back to the Big Island and collect Laura's ashes so I could have completion. I released her onto the wind and sea from a beautiful cliff overlooking the waves below.

The stress I was undergoing ignited a life-threatening condition called multiple myeloma, which I was harboring for the past ten years. My situation looked grim. My daughter Tassia and sister Bonnie flew out from the mainland and, along with Cyndi, a close friend, came to the conclusion I would be leaving this world to join Laura on the other side of the veil that separates our illusionary man-made reality from the true reality of love.

Arrangements were made to close down my residence and dispense of all my belongings and possessions. Priority Care Hawaii, my only source of income, also came to a halt. Everything in my life that was familiar instantaneously vanished, similar to the illusions that appear and then disappear in the performance of a magic trick. My slate was wiped clean. The only thing that remained for me was my illness and the foggy memory of what was. I had surrendered completely to the divinity of the process and embraced what was yet to come, trusting that the universe will guide me to my next step in this life-shifting experience.

> Being in human form allows us to physically
> experience the feeling and rapture of love.

We are coauthors of the characters cast in the live stage production of *The Road to Oneness*, now playing in the Theater of Miracles. We are here and now cast in this play to be at our highest potential of divine expression and celebrate our unity with all of creation. There is zero method of what experience is preferable to another. It is all experience. It is the journey we chose on our personal paths to Oneness. This is the nature of the process.

Over the next few weeks, I miraculously became stable, and the doctors felt that they had done what they could for me. I was discharged from the hospital. What was I to do? How was I going to take care of my medical or personal needs? I was alone on an island, bedridden, had very little strength, and was confined to either a wheelchair or walker. Laura my wife, soul mate and only family on the Island was gone. These challenging circumstances provided an opportunity that led to the door of an *initiation* that welcomed my continual spiritual growth.

When we focus our attention on the challenges, concerns, fears, and difficulties of our daily living, we become the point of attraction to the very thing we are trying to avoid. Our focus of attention best serves us when our awareness is upon our state of *Being* instead of acts of *doing*. That is how the universe works. The experiences that were presented to me were a reflection of the energies that I was projecting outwardly. When I shifted my attention and connected to the Oneness of my divine self, the circumstances that surrounded me also shifted accordingly. This is the experience and state of consciousness known as *Enlightenment*.

The loving intent behind my choices and the harmony in my surrendering into the arms of divine trust played an integral part in my healing. In the *acceptance* of my new character role and the *devotion* to express myself at my highest possible potential, I opened the gift of infinite possibilities.

Reflections

Inspirations Ignited by the Soul

*"I radiate the pure state of joyousness with each step
as I restructure the direction of my journey"*

The eternal flame of love burns within all of us. It is reflective in the joy and wonderment that is evident in a newborn or the innocent laugh of a child in celebration of his discoveries as he embraces the miracle of life.

Becoming aware of the truth that we are Pure Joy, Pure Love, is the beginning of our journey into a New Reality; the sacred place where harmony, peace, balance and love all reside.

Take a few moments to reflect on some of the beautiful events in your life that put a smile on your face. Become conscious of the feeling of joy and love flowing easily through you from your inner being, radiating from the flame within. That pure state of joyousness is who you truly are.

Day Four

Perception

It is intriguing that science affirms that everything in the universe is in a state of vibrational movement, and *change* is the only constant. Therefore, we will always be in the face of change. We are being given the opportunity to be open to the possibilities and miracles that the movement presents. It is a gift, a blessing for the emergence of the divinity within, to reveal an exalted and celebrated experience of transformation. In this state of consciousness, we can choose to view life from the eyes of the heart, embracing trust in the void of knowing what is yet to come.

The ego–mind takes into account the universal law of change as it weaves the stories that initiate the illusions of fear and our perceived separation from love. The play was written so credibly and our identification with the drama is so authentic that we believe it to be our reality.

> The answer to all our questions starts with the key question:
> "Who am I?"

I first became aware of the contrast between the ego-mind and the heart in my late fifties. After many years of devotion and practice, which is what I call *the work*, I am now able, for the most part, to spot the illusions and disguises of the ego much sooner than prior to becoming aware of the deceitful tenant that lived within my mind.

In order to appreciate the experience of joy, it is necessary to first take the road that leads to the depth of being in a place of darkness, separated and opposite from the light, or source energy. It is in this separation from love that duality resides—a world of contrasts, a world of experiences, and a vital tool of creation.

Change creates a world that always presents us with the opportunity to spiritually grow, embrace, and celebrate the essence of our truth, wisdom, and divine love. The eternal well of consciousness that dwells deep within our hearts waits silently in trust for our discovery.

When I perceived an experience emanating from heart-centeredness, all my feelings of joy, trust, compassion, and beauty fell under the umbrella of love. However, when I listened and contemplated the stories that were told by the greatest storyteller of all time, the Hans Christian Andersen of the body, the *ego-mind*, I had a completely different experience. This master impersonator, who disguises himself as our friend, is skillful in creating narratives filled with the uncertainty of change and the impermanence of life that are emotionally charged and perceived as thrillers—tales of conflict, revenge, jealousy, anger, resentment, or fear.

> *It is in the observing of our thoughts that we can begin the process toward a higher consciousness.*

My work at this point was to train and alert my mind to spot the illusions or the stories created by the ego-mind. I practiced being aware of the moments when I was disconnected from wisdom, truth, or source energy. It's easier to know when we are separated from consciousness because we get to experience the low vibration of an emotion in the form of fear, in exclusion of the wonderful feeling of a higher frequency associated with joy. Pay attention to the body; it's your instrument panel. Stay centered in the present moment. Train the ego to serve rather than allowing it to yield to its demanding self. I became consciously aware to stay focused from the perspective of the heart, knowing that it will always illuminate the darkness and light the way for me to see the truth.

If our civilization and planet are to flourish in the times to come, then it is imperative that we start to take conscious action from a new perspective other than the one that created the problem in the beginning. It is difficult to stay in harmony when we think that we are our minds, the masters of deception, questions, stories, and the creators of duality. Our mind is the main source of human suffering.

We all have our own personal truths and realities—the "I "we take ourselves to be. Based on our conditioning, association, and identification with the creative nature of the ego, our beliefs fabricated by the storyteller become our identities and our minds the controllers of our realities.

The full expression of our divine essence can only be realized when we accept all the aspects of our humanness, including the ones that our ego wants to keep hidden. The experience of realizing the self happens in its own time and in its own way. This state of *Being* is already there, fully manifested within us.

Because everything is in a constant state of change and constantly moving, we are always subject to the elusiveness of the future unless we detach from the outcome of the story. What could be more changeable than our thoughts and, consequently, our experiences? It is easy to now see why attachment creates fear and struggle. The meaning we give to the perceptions of our experiences is the root of all emotional pain. The wisdom we seek at this point in our lives is founded upon a world of spirit other than the calculating mind. It is only when we believe things to be permanent that we shut off the possibility to learn from change. It is from our choice to trust heart-intelligence, which often defies logic that creates the experience for embracing change and transformation.

Life unfolds as the spontaneous expression arising from the Oneness of the divine creation. The storyteller's role is meaningless because life simply *is*. When the mind is aligned with the heart, the body will dance naturally to the rhythm of the moment. Realizing our true being, in all its naturalness, is the blessing as we embrace the Buddha within.

> *When we focus upon our state of Being rather than on the circumstances, our reality changes.*

Our world has always been about change. But until this time in our evolution of the human species, the experience of change has occurred very slowly. It was immeasurable and provided the illusion that we were in a static period of development.

As we allow ourselves to become more conscious of the transition and process that we are now experiencing, we begin to realize that there is one goal in the reality we consider to be our lives. That observation is the awareness of Oneness—the embodiment of divine essence—toward which our journeys are leading us.

Under the radical changes that we are experiencing at this time in the evolution of consciousness, everything that we were conditioned toward or everything that seemed familiar is falling away. What will be is yet to come. We are in the process of free fall. Things will be different from these times forward in terms of what we might have believed, at the beginning, would be our lifestyle. All we have to do is look at our planet and the lives and challenges facing the people of this civilization. Extreme change in every aspect of existence is around us. What seems to be a world of chaos is actually the reconstruction of a new perspective that reflects living in a dimension that supports our true nature—that of love.

> *The lesson is always the purpose of the experience.*
> *The experience is always the reality of the perception.*

When we look at our lives and the world as we are now recognizing it to be, it is obvious that the playing rules have changed in a life-altering way. In order to transcend the past and ride the crest of the evolutionary divine wave, we have to shift our perception on what is truly valued. A life choice that emanates from the heart and resonates with the momentum of that change is required. We have to trust the divinity of the unfolding process of the creation. It is in this courage that we find the reflection of our devotion to self.

-- The possibilities and miracles we seek
reside in the abyss of the unknown. --

Reflections

Inspirations Ignited by the Soul

*"As I see the world through the eyes of love consciousness,
I experience the life I was born to live"*

Perception is how we experience our world. It dictates our state of mind and what character we play in the story the ego-mind has woven.

It is up to us to choose between illusion or Truth. However, to choose one is to surrender the other. The one you elect depends on what you value more, slavery or freedom.

As we shift our state of mind away from the veil of illusion we get to experience the "Real World"; a world of eternal possibilities and miracles; a place where life is looked upon in celebration.

See the world through the eyes of Love Consciousness and experience the life you were born to live.

Day Five

The Ego-Mind

In my innate yearning for love, I have listened to many CDs, gone to numerous workshops, read the many books that just fell into my lap, and even sat with masters and gurus. I was searching for happiness, for joy, and for love; it was my greatest quest to be consciously connected to source energy and to bathe in its light. It took time before I was able to intellectualize and understand what it is that I was reading and discovering. The actuality of being able to experience the feelings or live the understandings continued to elude me. I can just imagine what my life would be like now if all that I explored were manifested permanently in my reality at that time.

I will share with you that after many years of peeling away the illusions that held me captive to my mind, I still had a question that eventually would give rise to insights that would help me navigate the currents of the wind. The answer to that question freed me to experience the Oneness we were all born to celebrate. The question was this: Why does mankind have a resistance toward *change* and view the inevitability as an uncomfortable and frightening experience?

Simply put, it is all about the "I" and the continued survival or death of the ego. It is in our false identity with the "I" and the ego's fear it will die that are the sources of our striving instead of thriving.

> *When we identify with the ego, we separate from the love of self.*

The ego's biggest entitlement, the one that connects us to its identity, is that it can give us power. This illusion of control that the ego-mind has us believing gives it credibility and strengthens its hold over us.

The single most vital step we can take on our journeys of enlightenment is to become aware of the voice that tries to connect our sense of self to that of the ego-mind. Every time we shift our focus to the silence or gap between our thoughts, the light of consciousness illuminates the darkness and allows the truth and core essence of our *Being* to be readily seen.

> *The ultimate question we need to ask ourselves is this:*
> *Who would* I *be when my mind is quiet from thought?*

Most of my younger years I lived in my head, making decisions based on the illusions I believed to be my reality. However, I was finding that I kept facing the same patterns and challengers that I was trying to avoid. By allowing myself to experience the depth of my feelings and by using my body's reactions as my dashboard and indicator to search my soul, I was able to release low-density vibrational chargers that were embedded in my energy field by my perceptions that I believed were true. I discovered that by bringing myself to the awareness of how my body was feeling rather than identifying with the stories that my mind had woven, I was able to recognize the storyteller for who it was. It took acknowledgement and then releasing the need to control my life situations and trusting in the sacredness of the source that emanates from the core of my own that allowed my experiences to start flowing with ease and harmony.

Surrendering the need to mastermind our life experiences allows us to start to reach deeper to a level where we *feel* rather than think and *know* rather than believe. At this point, we will have arrived at a place where we create the reality of which we truly can move forward and orchestrate scenarios that serve our highest intent.

Experiences prepare us for living our lives in harmony and alignment. They present the opportunity for us to make a choice between illusion and the divinity of creation. Choosing the reality of love places us in alignment with universal organization and creative intelligence, the life force energy or spirit, and the underlying consciousness from which it emerges. We are in Oneness with the divine. The physical body, inclusive of the mind, allows us to experience, embrace, express, and celebrate the perfection of our higher selves in the unity of all that is.

In the duality of this world, we have to go beyond the mind and beyond any resistance in order to heal. We have to go beyond just understanding and intellectualizing the words if we are to be and live the experience of love. It's beneficial to come to that conclusion, but how do we actually bring it into our reality? The ego-mind seems to always get in the way.

> *The sole purpose of the ego-mind is to separate*
> *us from the experience of joy and love.*

What happens when we first get something we have wanted for a long time? We finally receive it, and we become extremely happy and pleased. Then, what thought suddenly crops into our heads almost immediately after that? "What happens if I lose it or what if it ceases to materialize like it is supposed to?" That joy-deflating thought came from the ego-mind in its mission to keep us in darkness instead of the light. We soon discover and realize that our ego-mind appears to be something other than our friend; however, its presence provides us with the opportunity of duality, which gives us perception and allows the making of a choice between unloving and loving thoughts and actions.

The ego-mind is one of judgment; it discriminates, and it is habitual and conditioning. It is the master of *separating* and *rejecting* anything that will serve the purpose to connect us to our wisdom and self-love. It acts as a magician, proficient at creating the illusion of duality. The ego-mind schemes, creates needs and wants, manipulates, and flares up in anger. It enjoys the repetition of being sly, skeptical, distrustful, and vulnerable, and it sees itself as an ingenious expert at the game of deception. This creator of illusion and suffering is responsible for all our negative emotions and thoughts. Its insatiable appetite requires constant validation and confirmation of its existence. The ego-mind's survival rests on its stories that project fearful outcomes and deceptively perceived external circumstances that are delivered by the constant currents of the *winds of change*. In the Buddha way of living, the concept of life and death originates as a function of the mind. It is made known by the ego's negative perspective on almost everything and is associated with a story of impermanence or change.

The ego-mind is completely conditioned by the past. It is one of the greatest narrators of all time. It makes up stories based on what we associated or identified with as we were growing up. We were, as children, void of the ability to fully reason or analyze; therefore, we took everything literally and created stories and beliefs about ourselves that were based on false data and illusions. Those stories became our realities based on the perspective and understanding we had at the time of the experience. They went directly into the subconscious and became our programmed scripts. We fell short of being good enough or smart enough; we were too small, too fat, or perhaps just lazy. We were defined as the things we needed in order to feel complete instead of who we truly are in our perfection. Our ego-minds do such a great job that we believed the stories to be true. Therefore, based on the Law of Attraction, we draw into our lives the very experiences that are directly in a vibrational match to those false inner beliefs.

Even though we recognize and accept that the ego is 100 percent malicious and begin to see through the ego's deceit and lies, we are still hesitant to simply abandon it. Without the spiritual awareness and wisdom of the heart or the consciousness of our true identities that emanate from beyond the mind, we simply think we have no other alternative. As we gradually discover our real nature and integrate it into our lives, our innate truth is awakened and grows stronger and clearer. As we listen to and focus on our inner guidance, the voice that gently reminds us of the Oneness of creation, we are able to shift our perspective and free ourselves from the ego's negative emotions that took over and robbed us of our birthright of joy and celebration. Finally, we come to experience the presence of wisdom, joy, and love as our true identities.

> *If we dislike the way our lives are unfolding, then we have to start looking at how we are actually thinking and vibrating in relationship to our perception and subconscious programing.*

Changing negative thoughts to positive ones just creates conflict in the mind. However, by changing our inner programs and shifting our focus away from the mind to embracing the heart, we change our vibrations and points of attraction, positively affecting attitude, motivation, sleep, weight, relationships, confidence, tension, stress, and all our experiences. We acquire a deeper understanding to our true purposes in life and a new sense of freedom that brings us peace, joy, harmony, balance, health, and love.

Recognizing the Ego-Mind

I am outlining some of the characteristics of the ego-mind—the voice that lives in our heads. Remember that its job is to create the illusion of duality and separate us from experiencing joy. Pay attention to its commanding way, so you can recognize when you are being led to a place of deceit.

- The ego-minds' primary weapons are doubt and fear.
- The ego-mind wants us to identify and believe that what it tells us about ourselves is true.
- The ego-minds' claim to recognition is that it supposedly gives us power. It wants us to be loyal to it.
- The ego-mind wants us to make absolute fools of ourselves.
- The ego-mind rejects thoughts of a higher consciousness because it diminishes the existence of the ego itself.
- The ego-mind says, "Be anything other than who you really are." When we are open and express ourselves in truth, we are vulnerable, and the ego is wary of that.
- The ego-mind separates us from our truth and encourages seeking acceptance from others rather than embracing our divinity.
- The ego-mind likes to complain, blame, and be negative. Being right and making others or the situation wrong gives us a momentary and false feeling of superiority. Instead of strengthening our sense of self, in reality we are giving away our power and reinforcing the illusions of the ego.
- The ego-mind is the only part of us that can give us the experience of guilt, which means it is in command.
- The ego-mind believes that it is very shrewd and can direct the outcome to get what it wants.
- The ego-mind believes it can create a desirable condition or disperse of an objectionable one. However, instead of

attracting a desirable condition, it stops it from arising or it keeps it in its place.

- The ego-mind uses confrontation to create negativity.
- The ego-mind enjoys pointing a finger and blaming.
- The ego-mind wants us to identify ourselves with our minds, so it can own us.
- The ego-minds' purpose is to make us believe it is all-powerful and independent.
- The ego-minds' job is to create dramas that separate us from the experience of love.
- The ego-mind likes conflict. It creates all judgment and criticism.
- The ego-mind is the creator of the duality that separates us from love.
- The ego-mind uses jealousy as a tool to make us feel unloved.
- The ego-mind rejects equality. It is beyond its comprehension.
- The ego-mind is selfish and only cares about itself.
- To the ego-mind, the present moment is other than existent. Only the past and future are considered important.
- The ego-mind tethers us to the past through complaints and regrets.
- The ego–mind identifies itself when it expresses itself through words like I, me, and mine.
- The ego-mind has zero understanding of what it feels like to love.

Reflections

Inspirations Ignited by the Soul

*"Within me is everything that is perfect, radiating
through me and out into the world"*

What seems like disorder or chaos in our world is coming from our perception of what's happening. Our interpretation of what's happening is just that, an interpretation, a story created by our ego-mind to keep us in a state of dis-harmony. That's what the ego does. It separates us from the experience of Joy. It's primary function is to create the contrast in our life; the shadow of darkness that blocks the "Light".

Perfection radiates brilliance. Its vibration is one of Love. We are Love, simply because all of nature was created in perfection and Love. We are one with nature.

There is perfection in imperfection, completeness in incompleteness, order in chaos and Love in all.

I invite you to visit my website to receive a Free download of your Bonus copy of the workbook "Perceptions". This insightful, artistic and vibrantly activating adjunct to *Navigating The Winds of Change* presents the opportunity for you to embark on a journey of discovery that opens the door to expanding your awareness to the beauty of life and embracement of your true nature.

stevenmanatrink.com

Day Six

Inner Guidance

One of the first myths that I encountered along my journey was the idea that *emotions* and *feelings* are one and the same, both emanating from the mind. I realized that if the ego can claim this illusion as truth, then we have zero way of distinguishing between the ego shouting and the heart gently whispering. We tend to overlook that a choice exists. This puts us in a victim mentality.

It is essential to learn to distinguish between emotions and feelings if we want to shift our realities. When experiencing a sense of pleasure, fulfillment, or joy, which are heart-felt and of high vibration, we are in alignment with the *feeling* of love. If it is an emotional pain or conflict that we are sensing, then it is our emotions that are speaking, a function of the ego-mind that carries lower vibrational frequencies.

When we become conscious of our states of *Being*, only then can we realize that we have a choice of focus between what our DNA reads as either *toxic* or *nurturing*. A simple way to tell them apart is to recognize that emotions all come from the mind, and feelings stem from the *nurturing* of the heart: beauty, joy, passion, creativity, love, and trust.

> Emotions = Struggle/Striving
> Feelings = Celebration/Thriving

It is important to pay attention to and be conscious of our inner guidance system, as it is similar to the dashboard of a car. It gives us information that is vital to our ultimate performance. It alerts us to possible situations that can become problematic. There are warning lights that go on when something is not functioning properly. These indicators are called emotions and are labeled guilt, sadness, jealousy, fear, doubt, rejection, despair, anger, or worry. Become aware that every *emotion* has a story attached to it created by the storyteller— the mind.

Emotions are signals that let us know the way we are thinking or perceiving the situation is out of alignment and balance with harmony. They are low-density frequencies that warn us when we are off course to our destination of fulfillment, abundance, and liberation.

The emotional body is an aspect of what we are. Our experience of emotion is a result of the focus of our perceptions based on our linear thinking, which is the only way the mind functions. In contrast to the mind, love is abstract and is understood and embraced only by the heart.

Love Is Mindless

Our feeling-body is a key element of our very humanness. It is productive, in our spiritual growth, to acknowledge our emotions and to feel them fully and deeply. *However, our intentions should be focused on relinquishing our impulses of allowing the emotion to govern our responses.* It serves our best interest to become more aware of our *feelings* and to spend time with them. It is natural to move toward what feels good. It is in harmony with well-being and with the essence of who we are. Trusting our inner guidance system transports us to the depths of our beings and to the compass of our souls.

The powerful gift of feeling, which we all possess, reaches inward and is connected to our heart intelligence. All that we seek literally lies within us, in the DNA of our cells. However, most of us choose to pay little attention to it. Feelings are a sense embraced through a pathway that connects us to the inner guidance system—the voice from within and our deep reconnection to the divine essence.

Our inner guidance system holds the innate blueprint to all of creation. It is composed of the truths, wisdoms, and divine knowledge—the very essence of our *Being*. Our physical forms allow us to physically experience, embrace, and celebrate the gift of humanness. This pattern is embedded into the energy frequencies of the higher vibrations that are in tune with harmony, alignment, and joy.

It is our inner guidance that indicates whether we are allowing the fullness of the universe to flow through us or if we are resisting embracing the love that is our own state of divine presence.

The key lies in our awareness that it is best to trust our inner guidance systems in determining the direction of our choices and be less concerned with the input of the logical mind, which is conditioned to feed us factors that are fear-based.

Let us honor the timeless wisdom of the inner guidance system. It steers us along the path that leads to the essence of divine love. Embracing our inner sense in the midst of our physical world and all its diversions will always lead us to a more vibrant and radiant life.

> When we connect to inner wisdom, we are
> in alignment with all of creation.

Reflections

Inspirations Ignited by the Soul

*"I observe my state of balance and heart-centeredness
with the unity and Oneness of creation"*

During our usual daily activity, much of our valued time is dwelling in the past or projecting our fears into the future. However, when we rest our mind in a state of non-thought, while embracing our intentions rooted in Divine Consciousness, we are free of past deliberating stories or anxieties that are future based. In this sacred place of stillness and quietude, we can hear the whispers of the Heart gently guiding us in Wisdom and Love.

The Buddha culture has taught us to embrace a state of consciousness based in the present moment, where we observe our thoughts and feelings from a distance, absent from judgment. Practice being watchful of your state of mind, it paves the way for the next step in our path to the awakening to a new reality, one that lies beyond the mind.

Day Seven

The Power of Choice

Archeologists estimate that modern humans have been on Earth for about two hundred thousand years. However, only now have we reached a point of profound change in the consciousness of mankind.

Life is moving forward, dancing with the wind and harmonizing with the joy of creation. This is the dance that beckons in these times. It is this reality that we are capable of manifesting at the crossroads of our perceived world where we get to experience the liberation derived from detached outcome and to embody our divine connectedness to Oneness with all of creation.

When we make *deliberate choices* that emanate from the heart, the experience is key to our ability to progress through this stage of human evolution. Nonattachment to outcome is the intent of our work. This extent of awareness and the surrender to the divinity of the process is achieved when we stand on the very edge of our gravest fear and know, in that moment, there is zero to fear. This is what we have learned to call taking a *blind leap of faith*.

If we wish to live our lives in Oneness, it is necessary to manifest unity within our own *Beings*. The higher our inner vibrational energy that results from heart-focused intent, the greater the reality of love that we experience.

The life I have chosen has taken me down many winding roads, up hills, and through deep valleys. The view from the top of the mountain always gave me the perspective of what lies ahead, whereas the climb from the base had a limited view over the direction I could take. There were times I wondered if I was awake or if I was the dreamer. I experienced sadness that brought me to tears and, on the other hand, joys that erupted from deep within. My life was filled with contrast and duality. I knew from the many experiences and lessons that crossed my path that it was imperative to stay centered and grounded in the reality of the moment if I was to endure it all. I was being given the gift to apply and put into practice the essence of the lessons that I have been faced with from the time I choose to be upon this planet. This was the direction of my spiritual adventure—the core and perspective of the Buddhist way of being, living in the present moment while embracing change.

By choosing to be born into this world, we have been given the opportunity to experience the powerful force of change—the impermanence of life itself. At the same time, we have been provided with the blessed opportunity to also walk the path of joy and celebration.

The ancient wisdom of the Buddhist comes from the knowing that all attachment to what is moving away from us is the cause of all human struggle and suffering. How beautiful one's life can be if striving was absent from the equation and replaced with thriving. The attachment to results, outcome, or expectations sets us up for emotional distress and a feeling of powerlessness and vulnerability. All of which lead to something other than well-being, joy, and celebration.

Every human *Being* has been provided with empowering gifts that are oftentimes overlooked or taken for granted. One of the most inspiring is the power of choice brought about by change. What we choose to focus our attention on with *deliberate conscious intent,* versus what we attract into our experience blindly, becomes our realities and determines our well-being and vibrancy in every aspect of our lives.

We have a *choice* to differentiate every thought, action, and experience in conscious awareness. We have a choice between the perspective of the ego-mind that is designed to evoke separation from wisdom or the heart that embraces liberation. Our realities are a reflection of how we choose to perceive life. Looking through the eyes of the heart will always feel natural, easy, vibrant, and joyful.

The way we make choices in our daily lives is determined and experienced by the relationship we have with ourselves—how we value, appreciate, accept, and love who we really are. When we live from this level of consciousness, truth and wisdom become our guides and the awareness of choice our magic wands.

> Life is a journey of the heart.

I have discovered that there is a significant difference between making a *decision,* an intellectual function of the mind, which we usually deem as final and permanent, versus embracing the guidance that comes from the heart. A decision is based on understanding the facts at hand and is weighed by logic, practicality, and desired results; most importantly, it's rooted in fear-based projections.

However, when coming from the perspective of *choice,* we take into account the same assumed information, but also pay attention to our heart consciousness to direct us toward the action we need to take that is aligned and in harmony with the flow of wisdom and truth. When making a choice rather than a decision, we can always allow for adjustments and alter our course in the moment. The heart always leads us in the direction of love.

In the pages that follow, there is substantial opportunity to learn and embody the teachings and insights that are presented. It is in our devotion to ourselves that we will transcend the illusions and limitations of the reality created by our conditioning and perceptions constructed from false data.

Our experiences are either unloving or loving.

If we persist to see life from the perspective of the ego-mind, then we are continuing to invite the difficulties we are now experiencing by remaining in a state of energy imbalance. It would be preferable to choose from entering into any crucial situation in this unbalanced state. The outcome would feed and validate our fears and anxieties, creating more of the very thing we are striving to transcend.

At this point it would be wise to stop and bring forth our wisdom and insights that we were blessed with from our experiences or lessons. Applying them in our lives is the course of action that has to take place.

Over time, I learned to look for the insight, the gem, in the lesson that is to be found in every experience that life brings us. Leaving the drama of the story behind, I put the jewel in my pocket and moved forward in my journey, free from the anchor of the illusionary stories that bind me to an identity other than love.

In this world of duality or opposites, as we view things from two points of reference, we gain perspective: pain/pleasure, evil/good, failure/success, sad/joy, strive/thrive, death/life. The duality gives us an experiential reference point and the appreciation of the richness of choice that is found in dramatic contrasts. It is necessary that we experience the extremes in order to realize the divine foundation that underlies life.

Our thoughts are energy, and both perspectives in the duality carry a vibrational frequency with the exception that one holds a *higher* vibration and is in alignment with the energies of wisdom and truth that we as a species are in the mist of embracing in this lifetime. As we begin to view life from a new advantage sight, we can now realize the perfection the duality provides in our process of ascension.

Rather than being victims in the stories of our lives, we are fully responsible participants in the choices we are presented with along the way.

The duality/contrast that we experience in our lives gives us an opportunity to choose between the ego's low-density energy of limited perspective and the higher level of vibration emitted from the ancient wisdom of the heart. As we enter into this new energy and in order to continually experience the harmony, vibrancy, and joy in the real world, it is essential that we consciously choose heart-focused intent. Loving choices serve to dissipate the underlying lower vibrational energy that brings forth undesirable consequences. It also allows true objectivity to be possible, revealing the gift of the clarity that was there all along.

The energy or frequency of our vibrations is the vehicle that carries information. It is the source and the force, the essence of life. Its impetus stems from our intent.

As our civilization begins to awaken into a higher consciousness, we become more aware of the miracles of life. Everything that we perceive in our experiences is given shape by *thought,* created in our minds, and given *substance* by feeling in our hearts. A mind with heart fills life experience with love-based truth. The heart-mind-DNA connection is vital in attaining the empowerment of physical, emotional, and spiritual well-being. Our choice from the point of view of *devotion* would be to shift perception away from the illusions of the ego-mind and focus on the truth and wisdom that lives within our heart.

~~ *When perception is rooted in divinity, we experience life that allows us to soar in the reality of love.* ~~

Reflections

Inspirations Ignited by the Soul

*"I choose to see a world of Beauty and embrace
all my experiences as Joyous and Loving"*

Love is abundant in all of natures creations; the magnificent sunset painted on the canvas of a distant sky, the melodic song of the sparrow welcoming spring, the touch of a warm wind gently caressing your skin or the wonderful sweet fragrance of the blossoming red rose. This is the Real World, a world created from Love and observed through the heart. It is here that everything that happens is to raise our awareness to the Oneness and beauty of creation.

However, in the world of our mind-made reality our observation is through the eyes of ego-mind. This illusionary realm is where our perception of what's happening is based on our fears of the past or the projection of those worries into the future. Either way, in this arena of blame and fright, we are portrayed as the victim of circumstances and are powerless.

Our work in this moment is to start viewing the world through the lens of the Heart-Mind where we will find our life experiences to be Loving and Joyous. Be grateful for the opportunity of the lessons the Soul seeks for its growth. It is our gift from the universe. In this new perception of the Real World you find your loving-self.

Day Eight

Illusions

Thinking is a natural function of the human species. The majority of the population living on our planet is completely identified with the endless stream of mind chatter. It is this compulsive thinking that usually leads us to a place of confusion or conflict. The ego-mind is a master of stories that we *believe* are true. It is these stories that fashion our perceptions of reality, specifically the perception of a reality that convinces us that who we are is who we *think* we are. As long as we are emotionally involved in the story of I am who I think I am, we are attached to something that is transient and separates us from what is real. These stories and beliefs can trap us in our imaginations. The ego-mind's job is to create the illusion of duality in the real world of Oneness.

The storyteller's focus of "I" is always attached to the end result of its narratives: *I am a happy person*, or *I am a sad person*; *I am a success*, or *I am a failure*. But often, we are unaware that we consistently create, live, and identify with the stories and the false characters of the illusion that ultimately creates disharmony and disease. In our strong loyalty to the mind's perceived reality, we lose sight of the bigger picture, the reality that lies in the wisdom and truth of the heart.

The good news is that if you can recognize the mind's storytelling as an illusion, it dissolves and the story ends. The mind's survival depends on us mistaking an internal narrative for reality. It is in the *observing of our thoughts* that we can begin the process to a higher consciousness.

The mind's power to create associations is important. It is the way we make sense of reality as human *Beings*. We collect identities—I, me, mine—based on the ego-mind's function to possess and control. The ego wants us to identify and believe that we are our minds.

Science has confirmed that we live in a holographic universe. Everything is interconnected through universal consciousness and holds the entirety of the illusion in a three-dimensional reality. The complete blueprint for our existence is contained and is eternally accessible in each and every one of our cells. We are whole, holistic rather than the sum of our parts. Our hologram was designed to require energetic nourishment, of which the most essential form is the vibrational frequency of love. To live and thrive, our cells need to bathe in this conscious energy. All conscious changes made directly to our body-mind-spirit hologram have a profound and accelerated effect in healing. Literally, it is love that gives our cells life.

> *Conflicts lie outside of the wholeness.*

It is evident that the lower density of energy frequencies associated with the illusionary stories of the ego-mind compromise our immune system and affects the vibrancy of our lives. When we are focused from a vantage point of trust, compassion, joy, peace, creativity, passion, or love, which are higher levels of frequency that come from beyond the mind, we experience the celebration of life. These higher frequencies communicate to our DNA, data that is healing and nurturing. They contribute to our overall state of well-being. The expression of our DNA and its communication with the cells in our bodies are primarily determined by these frequencies.

The word *I* embodies the greatest error and the deepest truth. In normal everyday usage, "I" represents the ancient misperception of whom we are—an illusory sense of identity created from the ego's perspective of self. This illusory identity of who you think you are is what Albert Einstein, who had deep insights into the reality of space and time and also of human nature, referred to as "an optical illusion of consciousness." These collections of characters form our stories. Our perception of reality that comes from the mind becomes a reflection of the illusion that compromises our harmony, balance, and alignment.

Life as we once knew it is changing, and it is time to awaken to the integral part we play in the journey we have chosen to take in our evolution of humankind. Coming from our new perspective of "I *am*, therefore I think" rather than "I think, therefore I *am*," we have a responsibility to be conscious of our thoughts and make choices that only our hearts know to be true. It is the way to energetically detach from our stories, so we can live in the eternal present moment of love.

> *Struggle is to identify with the illusion.*

The world of sensory perception is the world of time, change, beginnings, and endings. It is variable in its interpretation. If each individual perceives the world based on his or her distinct perception of experiences, beliefs, environments, and senses, then everyone experiences the world and their reality differently. However, true reality is simply the embracing of the experience and the feeling of love. It is based on a universal truth that always remains the same, regardless of what we think or believe. It is naturally sensed and always consistent, gentle, and kind. Love emanates from beyond the mind and is the only constant in our ever-changing world of perceptions and illusions. It applies to everything that nature created and transcends time; everything else is an illusionary story fabricated by the ego.

If our race is to thrive and flourish, then humanity needs to align itself through the cohesiveness of truth, love, and wisdom. We need to play, as children in the eternal garden, the game of hide-and-seek, always looking for the gem hidden in our reality of the illusion.

Everything the mind perceives, in the absence of the heart, is the illusion. When we think of distressing things, we sense fear. When we are fully engrossed in a movie, our emotions are experienced as real, even though we know it is all just a show.

The beautiful thing about illusions is that they are critical windows into the mind. They help us realize that things are never what they seem, but also that our experiences of the world shape our understanding of them.

~~ The mind enjoys feeding on the illusions of self ~~

Reflections

Inspirations Ignited by the Soul

"As I surrender the illusion of fear, my mind is at peace"

An illusion is a story that our ego-mind has created to take you away from the experience of freedom. It is our disconnection from the presence of the "Light": Love & Joy.

Any story that causes you a reaction other than the feeling of peace, is fear based. It comes from the greatest storyteller of all time, the Hans Christen Anderson of the body, the ego-mind.

The illusion is playing on the stage in the theater of the mind and appears real only in the darkness and shadows of the past or the imaginary projection of the future. It comes from our basic lack of trust and the result of negative perception.

What stories are you holding on to? Are you ready to let go of the illusionary dramas that are compromising your inner peace? Give yourself permission to surrender to harmony, knowing that divine guidance is always with you. The present moment is the only place where you can live in peace.

Day Nine

Truth

Everyone is unique with an expression and a life purpose that is specific to him or her. Therefore, our personal truth is different for each one of us. We find our *individual* truth as we listen to and follow our hearts. However, there is only one universal truth: the universal truth of love, and it exists in all creation. This is the truth that I refer to in these writings and the one I am continually revealing within myself.

> The truth we seek is found within ourselves.

The most loving choice in how we will experience our lives is the way we embrace trust and the divinity of it all. The magnitude to which we trust in the universe is in how conscious and aware we are about truth. They go hand in hand, connected as one with each other. This is the work we are asked to embody in our journeys so that it becomes a joyous reflection of the higher energies, which we are seeking as an essential part of our realignment process.

When I recognized the level of connectedness with my very own heart and the opportunity to experience the love that was harbored there, I had taken my first step toward the blind leap of faith that I had been resisting throughout my life. I surrendered to the fear of the void, the emptiness of thought, and the experience of free falling by releasing, detaching, and surrendering control and outcome. I found it important to acknowledge myself for the progress I was making on my soul's journey; it reflected courage to release the need to control. By consciously shifting my intent to *allowing*, I enhanced the opportunity to manifest the highest possible outcome for myself and experience a state of *Being* in alignment to Oneness.

As I became more aware of the lessons that the winds of change were presenting to me, I realized how the contrast in my life played an important part in the equation. It perpetuated truth and the awakening to wisdom consciousness. The contrast brought me to a new awareness, even though it may have been through pain and suffering, just as a fever brings you to the alertness that something in your body is out of harmony. Truth is always connected to wisdom and, therefore, to universal intelligence. Wisdom resides in the silence of our minds—the gap between our thoughts.

Let us take a look at truth and recognize that it excludes mental ideas or the judgment that something is right or wrong. Truth is neither good nor bad. Only good exists in the universe. If you find a particular piece of artwork distasteful, it could still be recognized as a work of art. The truth I am referring to rests on a different type of evidence that is nonmaterial or scientifically proven. It is way beyond mind-made reality. It is in the all-knowing of a force that is greater than the creation of our minds. *Truth is the secure trust in the divine creative intelligence of the universe and the acceptance of God's will.* The truth creates a connection and knowingness. It allows us to express and be at our fullest potential, empowering our lives.

> Truth is a consciousness that is guided by spiritual wisdom.

In order to experience the truth, we must live our lives with courage, trust, transparency, integrity, and authenticity. Our words must always be congruent with our actions. Congruent people can always be trusted. They say what they mean. All loving behavior toward others comes from inner congruence, which requires that we love, honor, and be truthful to ourselves. In truth, everything is in perfect order. Truth is always liberating; it sets us free. It is the only consciousness that will allow us the joy of the present moment.

All mental suffering and, consequently, physical suffering is caused by the identification, imagination, and negative habits of the thinking process of the ego-mind—the most magnificent storyteller of all time. The illusions first show up as indicators called emotions and manifest as contrast, shadows, or adverse circumstances that we create in our lives. We have zero control over the thoughts that come into our minds, but what we can do is shift our perception of the experience we are being presented. When we become more aware that the emotional pain is caused by the illusions created by our minds, we can choose to surrender the thoughts that created the emotion. Therefore, by recognizing and rejecting the illusion, we automatically become aware of the truth. With practice, we become more conscious when our minds get in the way of the experience of joy and peace, knowing that love is always present.

> Trusting the divinity of the process of life by
> seeking the truth from within shows us that
> our external lives are only a dream.

It took me constantly processing my thoughts over time and looking at every situation from a higher perspective of a spiritual reality to notice a shift in energies and the connection to my core essence. Remember, in all cases, the universe sets you up to succeed. Giving ourselves permission to move through our challenges and welcome the *initiations* allows us to discover what already exists within.

When we succeed in shedding ourselves of everything that supported our mind-made realities, the illusions skillfully masterminded by the ego, we are ready to begin to understand a new perception of a reality that is absolute. The power of the conscious understanding of what is real and what are the illusions that we perceive as real can only be verified by how it internally feels to us. We begin to rely more on our own inner guidance systems to navigate through the unchartered winds of change in order to glide and soar on the currents of life.

~~ Change is the movement of life, conducted by the soul of creation, played by the orchestra of truth ~~

Reflections

Inspirations Ignited by the Soul

"I always have a choice between truth or illusion. Truth always brings me peace"

Truth is a consciousness that is guided by spiritual wisdom. It is the secure belief in the "Divine Creative Intelligence of the Universe" and the acceptance of "God's" will. The truth creates a connection and knowingness, and that in turn creates our state of being.

Truth, unlike beliefs never changes or waivers; it is the universal law forever encoded in the infinite dream of reality. Our mind has a challenge comprehending truth because it is beyond reason or logic.

Our most basic choice about how we will experience our life is to what extent to we trust the divinity of the universe and how conscious and aware we are about truth. They go hand in hand. They can only exist together.

Give yourself permission to move through your challenges by embracing the wisdom and truth of the universal consciousness. Discover what already exists within you. Remember we can always choose what feels "Loving". It will guide you on a path to a greater awareness. The world and your place within it will shift.

Your Bonus copy of "Perceptions" the workbook that aligns with *Navigating The Winds of Change* is available for a Free download. Simply go to my website to instantly receive your Bonus copy of "Perceptions", the artistic workbook that supports your journey into a new a reality.

stevenmanatrink.com

Day Ten

Initiation

We live in a universe of constant change. The mind likes comfort and enjoys knowing what is next in order to control the outcome so it can make us feel safe and secure. We have been conditioned to believe our perceived experiences and their related consequences are real. In believing this illusion, we arrive to the deceptive conclusion that we really do have control.

In navigating the path that change has presented me, I was continually faced with the mind's intervention wanting to know what will come next. Stress, anxiety, doubt, and conflict were all underlined with the fear of losing control and became a part in the play that kept me on edge. The perception of uncertainty created an imbalance and usually caused me to spin out of control. "Why is this happening to me?" was a question that had arisen time and again. I looked to blame, to find a logical reason or to do anything other than to accept the responsibility that I had written this experience into my life. I was faced with the challenge of how to change the situation and correct it. In essence, I was given an opportunity to spiritually grow.

It became apparent that if I wanted to experience a different result than the repeated destructive pattern I always seemed to end up with, I would have to redirect my focus and take action from another perspective. I realized that my reality was based on my perception at the time and how I was viewing the experience.

If anything were to be different, then my perception would have to change.

The word *challenge* needs to be restructured. As long as we see what's happening as a challenge, we will be viewing it from the point of a task, restraint, or undertaking. The low-density vibration related to our perceptions of fear compromises our inner vibrations—the point of attraction that is reflected in our experiences. This results in us launching an assault to face up to and move past the challenge in order to achieve our goals.

Our thoughts, words, and perceptions translate into vibrational frequencies. The expression of our DNA and its communication with the cells in our bodies are primarily determined by these frequencies generated and based on the way we view ourselves, our thoughts, and our beliefs, as well as our environments.

Now, let's look at it from a higher place. Instead of interpreting the experience as a challenge, we are going to shift our perspective and view it as an *initiation*.

An initiation is an event that ultimately welcomes us into a new awareness.

Initiation is different than being admitted into a club or a part of a ritual. It is an event that welcomes us into a new reality. It is an experience that allows us to see ourselves from the perspective of the liberation from duality into the embracement of Oneness simply by observing the experience as something that is happening *for us* rather than happening *to us*. It marks the death of our old selves and the rejoicing birth into a new awareness, another evolution in our journeys. How the experience is received from the perspective of a challenge versus an initiation is the difference between *striving* and *thriving.*

Initiations are signposts that we have written into our scripts. We have placed them in our paths strategically so we would be able to embody the gems found in the lessons of our process of transformation. They are truly gifts.

The word *challenge* and its corresponding association with resistance, obstacle, or uncertainty carries a lower vibrational frequency than the word *initiation.* I am referring to a welcoming of a new perspective; a reality that leads to personal growth and the liberation from being tethered to an old story. Initiation opens the gates to a life filled with harmony, alignment, and vibrant health.

Applying and integrating the knowledge of epigenetics into our daily lives by purely choosing uplifting and higher vibrational thoughts, words, or actions supports and enhances the mind-body-spirit connection. It frees us from our emotional conflicts and challenges and puts us more in alignment with divine consciousness.

To be conscious that I had a choice between my point of focus in every thought, action, and experience that I encountered was the blessing, the gift of a lifetime. It allowed me to energetically detach from my stories, so I could live in the present moment of harmony, truth, and joy.

Once I had transcended and embraced my new awareness of the purpose of my experiences or the changes that were taking place in my life, I began to sustain that perspective of my new reality. I became aware that the lower density energies that I have been accustomed to experiencing were absent from my new perception of reality. I distinctly remember the morning I woke up and felt that something was missing from my life: **drama**. I then realized the gift and value of *initiation*.

Our objective in this moment of awareness is to choose what defies understanding and then direct our focus to the love, wisdom, and truth, which originate from beyond the mind. It is at this time we begin to reach out to the ever-expanding possibilities of this world of wonder and our place within it, simply by shifting our perception away from the illusions of the ego-mind and towards embracing the universal consciousness that lives within our hearts.

~~ The key to experiencing liberation centers upon our willingness to embrace love and the celebration of Oneness ~~

Reflections

Inspirations Ignited by the Soul

*"I accept what my experience brings me as
the purpose of the experience"*

Become the observer of the play that is unfolding before you. From a Higher perspective, watch what is happening on the stage you are playing on. Pay attention to the characters; watch the experience that you are having in this moment. Be the witness with zero judgment, zero meaning. Just watch, be still, observe. Accept the experience for the gift it is.

Every person that comes into our life, every situation we encounter, every experience that we have is Divine. It's the dance of the universe on the Winds of Synchronicity.

Look for the messages, pay attention to the lesson and seek the purpose of the experience. It is all happening *for us*, other than *to us*. Every experience brings our awareness, our consciousness, to a Higher level. Begin to see past the stories or illusions of the ego-mind, to the home we never left, as we awake from the dream, in our journey of self-discovery.

From this "Higher" balcony viewpoint of our play, make choices that will serve your Highest good, your greater purpose, choices that are rooted in Love Consciousness. Your experiences will then reflect the beauty of your dream and the unfolding creation of your journey into self-realization.

Day Eleven

Oneness

The focus of spiritual growth is on the journey itself rather than the destination. The realization of Oneness, which is the experience and culmination of the process we are experiencing, is the universal golden thread that is woven throughout the tapestry of all creation. *It is our divine essence and the full expression of our heightened state of Being*—the knowingness of our own inner guides and the divine connection to creative intelligence. We are all connected in Oneness as the rock is to the mountain from which it came. The rock holds within it the soul of the mountain.

Oneness
*The eternal energy, the pulse, and driving force
of creation that flows through all life.*

As I journeyed over the past years into the transformational process, guided by the changes in my life circumstances, I was led to a new realm of awareness. I found that it became easier to determine where I stood along the way at any point, simply by becoming aware of the ease or difficulty in the experience of manifesting my heart's desire in my day-to-day life. I realized that I was able to be the observer and the object of that awareness at the same time. I became aware of any judgment that my ego created. The process of taking responsibly for my state of *Being*, the evaluating and choosing loving

Steven Mana Trink

and nourishing thoughts and actions, became a vital part of my life. This practice of being aware was supported by my focused intent. All my thoughts, actions, and choices of loving intention contributed to the manifestation of my new reality and the experiences that I attracted into my life.

When we sense a separation from our divine connectedness, then we are identifying with the illusions and stories of the mind. Oneness is who we truly are in a world of unity that reflects and embraces our vibrational frequency and energy of love.

> *Oneness is the presence of absolute awareness*
> *transcending perspective.*

I have come to recognize that in this lifetime we stand at the threshold of a grand adventure. In order for us to be able to completely shift our perception of a reality that binds us to the ego-mind's illusions that have held us back since birth, we need to replace that structure of perception with a new realm of conscious awareness that transcends our physical senses and shifts our focus to heart-centeredness.

Consciousness is a choice that deepens the connection with all aspects of our *Being*. It allows us to experience the celebration of life that presents itself in the divine order of perfection. We need to trust the process of the merging and integration of self at each level and embrace it with loving intent. When we become aware of the unfolding story of the reality of Oneness, we get to experience all that we truly are.

> *Oneness is the essence of our own divinity.*

Consciousness is an identity in the unity of all that is, the ultimate end result of ascension. When our vibrational frequency is in unity to the higher resonance of source energy, we are able to easily determine our course of navigation in manifesting outcomes that are in balance, alignment, and harmony with the divinity of the creation.

At this time in the evolution of our species, humankind as a collective consciousness is in the process of revealing, embracing, and integrating into its daily life the wisdom and universal truths with which it has been blessed. We have been given the opportunity to both experience and surrender to the limitations and fears we embody, resulting from the separation of self that the ego has so cunningly conditioned us to believe is who we are. The Oneness toward which we are working is the energy that fuels the momentum of the radical changes that are taking place on this planet in this phase of our journeys.

It is in our *highest* purpose that we recognize the patterns of self-defeating conditioning by the ego's perception of self. Shifting our perception of the resulting low-density frequencies to a higher vibration reflecting our true selves is now our primary focused intent.

The possibilities of what can be created and experienced in this lifetime are infinite and abundant. There is only joy and celebration to be experienced when we unite in Oneness with oneself. It is our embracement of *self-love* that marks our completion of this phase in our journeys of enlightenment.

The precious gift the soul gives itself lies in the experience of embracing our own divinity, the embodiment of love in the physical form. It is a gift to be cherished. The key rests upon our willingness to acknowledge our divine essence and to come to experience—in Oneness—the reality of love.

> *Ultimately, we discover ourselves to be Oneness.*

Reflections

Inspirations Ignited by the Soul

*"I am moving forward, dancing with the wind and
harmonizing with the joy of life in every breath"*

The key to all we would accomplish in this lifetime centers upon our
willingness to embrace all that we are, for the chance that we may
come to experience – in Oneness – all that we truly Are.

A vast inter-dimensional conversion in consciousness is presently
transpiring throughout creation. As we experience these shifts
and the energies carry us to ever-higher levels of awareness, our
attunement to the higher frequencies becomes stabilized.

Know that we are in command of our situation at all times. We are
able to choose to step back, at will, from the heat of the moment
and make the conscious choice to shift our energy to one emanating
from the place of heart-centeredness.

The energy of Love we consciously project onto any moment or
situation shifts the outcome to one that will give you a more valued
result. By embodying this training, our life becomes one directed by
intention rather than the unconscious reflection of chance.

Recognizing the power to create your reality is your key to turning
the page and beginning a new chapter in your own life story.

Day Twelve

Celebration

Finally, we have arrived at the threshold embarking on our way out of the maze of illusions that separate us from the truth and pure love of our *Being*. We are ready to leave behind the mind, the creator and interpreter of the illusion, to discover the pure and absolute nature within.

When we bathe in the liberation that comes from detachment to outcome, we will be able to secure the divine consciousness of love. Our changes in perception that take place in the awareness of the detachment from results, free us from the grasping mind and the false sense of security of our illusionary stories.

Contemplating the freedom of detachment from what the mind has trapped us to believe is familiar and safe is only part of the process. It now takes the courage of applying and integrating the new understandings, insights, and wisdom that change brings into our daily lives. It is only then that we get the opportunity to experience the shift that takes place—our perception is reflective of our new reality of liberation.

All the changes that are taking place in our individual worlds are the sole opportunities for us to assess a new way of perceiving our lives. It becomes a new reality that is observed from the vantage point of a higher vibrational frequency rather than from the world we are ascending from and the old frequencies it was built on.

Our journey is an experience that we, as Human Beings, are simply here to embrace and celebrate—to participate from our inherited wisdom and follow the inner voice that guides with love. It's that simple!

The enhancement of our vibrations is key to what we wish to accomplish in this transitional time. When we observe with conscious awareness the energy we bring to any situation, we make the highest possible contribution to the well-being of all.

> *When our perception is rooted in illusion,*
> *we experience a fear-based reality.*

Because our thoughts are energy, our perspectives carry a vibrational frequency. Thoughts associated with the unity of Oneness carry a higher vibrational energy helping to facilitate the shift that is taking place in global consciousness: the remembering of the universal truth that we are all one love.

Instead of becoming a victim of the stories of our lives, we stand as fully responsible participants in making choices that support our highest potentials. The duality/contrast that we experience in our lives gives us an opportunity of choice between the ego's low-density energy of limited perspective and the higher level of vibration emitted from the ancient wisdom of the heart. As we emerge into this new energy and in order to continually experience the harmony, vibrancy, and joy in the real world, it is essential that we consciously choose heart–focused intent. In doing so, we dissipate the underlying lower vibrational energy that brings forth undesirable consequences. Furthermore, this choice allows true objectivity to be possible.

Step into the creation that was always my welcome,
My spirit guides spoke the words so well:
The miracle has already been created,
Embrace the moment from the heart,
Trust the wisdom of the perfection,
All is divine.

We have chosen to experience humanness in order to taste and embody the exquisite feelings of divine connectedness. The profound realization of peace and inner stillness and the sense of awareness that we discover ourselves to be is our ultimate goal in the embodiment of Oneness.

-- Striving comes from a consciousness of lack.
Thriving is living in the abundance of love --

Reflections

Inspirations Ignited by the Soul

"In every breath I take, I am aware that the joy of the adventure of life is found in the embracing of the moment".

We can only celebrate in the moment of Now. It is where everything takes place. Zero exists outside of it. Each moment opens the door allowing the experience of all adventure to unfold.

The painter derives his Joy from the process of the creation with each stroke he takes; the carpenter hitting one nail at a time; the singer, one with his music and song.

When we are present in the celebration of "Now" there is only Joyousness.

Our work is to train our mind to watch our mind, to spot when we are focused on something in the past or future. With practice we get to see how awareness illuminates the darkness and "Lights" the way for us to embrace the celebration.

The Celebration and Joy, in our adventure of life is in the moment where the illusion fades and our dance with Love begins.

Day Thirteen

Devotion

The embracement of the love of self bypasses the mental process. It is where we fully surrender to our hearts and souls. It is the leaving behind of all the trappings of our identities. Ultimately, it is the embodiment and total recognition of the core of our divinity that resides within us and in every expression of life, throughout all of creation.

> *Love of self is expressed through our heart-felt choices.*

The way we go about accomplishing our objectives in our daily lives is determined and experienced by the relationship we have with ourselves—how we value, appreciate, and love who we really are.

Our physical world of form itself is an illusion or an effect we perceive, initiated by the vibrational frequency of energy set in motion from the decisions or choices we make between viewing life either through the dark lenses of the ego-mind or from the loving eyes of the heart. One creates a resistance to achieving our goals, while the other welcomes, accepts, and embraces the experience. Both viewpoints create our beliefs, thoughts, attitudes, emotions, or feelings. All of our experiences are a reflection of how we perceive the life we are attracting. Choosing from the perspective of the heart always feels natural, easy, vibrant, and joyful.

When we acknowledge the power of love, the divine essence that resides within, we begin to see experiences as a way to nurture and empower the unfolding stories of our lives. Self-love is at the very core of our well-being, joy, and self-empowerment, as well as our ability to create, embrace, and celebrate an abundant life.

I started to look deeper into the lessons and blessings that each experience brought me and became aware of the *gems* I was given. Each experience allowed me the perspective of choosing from heart-centeredness rather than from the controlling, dictating mind. I found that the opportunity invited me into a new realm of awareness. My experiences reflected a higher vibration and hence a more harmonious and loving reality.

Choosing devotion (self-love, wisdom, and divine knowledge) instead of discipline (willpower or fear-based thinking of the linear mind) is a way for us to move out of victimhood and into mastery over our radiance, vibrancy, and well-being. Our attitudes take on another perspective. Instead of resistance and struggle, we flow in concert to our self-embracement. It is easy and effortless. Joy is a natural state of *Being* and resonates at the highest level of frequency of any epigenetic influence. By shifting our choice of living our lives from a viewpoint of willpower and discipline to a perspective of nurture and lovingness brings about a simpler approach, one that is performed and experienced in celebration.

When we attempt to discipline ourselves to follow a specific program or complete a specific intention, we usually wind up leaving or discontinuing the agenda based on a logical reason. The mind likes reasons because it controls through reason. It usually comes up with some very good arguments to end the struggle we seem to have with discipline, willpower, or fear. In the end, the ego perceives the situation as a failure. The ego-mind is an energy-draining and self-fulfilling mechanism that tries to accomplish a result that is motivated out of something other than a loving act.

Goals can be easy, enjoyable, and health supporting—simply by shifting our perceptions of how we observe ourselves in the relationship to the experience. Telling ourselves repeatedly that it is a good thing or reciting affirmations will fall short of giving us positive results. Intellectualizing or conceptualizing is a mind function, and our motivation comes from reason, which is usually backed by a need or fear that holds low-density vibrations that compromise harmony within our bodies. However, the most powerful motivational source—one that carries a high vibrational frequency—is the one of devotion. It stems from the heart rather than the mind. It is our divine connection.

By simply turning our focus inward towards our heart-centeredness, we are able to feel and embody our divine connections. The embracement of this experience of Oneness allows us to access and implement the most powerful motivational tool: *love*. From this platform all goals become easy and effortless.

> *You yourself, as much as anybody in the entire universe,*
> *deserve your love and affection.*
> ~ Siddhartha Gautama Buddha ~

Devotion is empowering and facilitates dissolving the resistance to healing and embracing love. It supports the choice to awaken to and live in the reality of a new consciousness. The objective of approaching our lives in devotion is to transcend the illusions of the limiting mind and resonate in harmony and balance with the movements of life.

Tune in to the music that plays from the heart. Listen to the songs of guiding intuition. The symphony of life is the music of eternity, and dancing to the beat that embraces love is our destiny. Now is our time to take the next step in the dance of life, one that is based on our *devotion* to a new way of living.

Reflections

Inspirations Ignited by the Soul

"I am blessed and therefore I see the world in the "Light of Love."

Love, Joy and Peace lives within us.
The "Light" is who we are.
Illusions can cover it, but it will always shine.

The meaning of Love lies within itself. It is forever etched in our Heart. We recognize this when our perception of ourselves reflects the purity of the Creation.

Being a Child of the Universe, One with Nature, we are the Miracle of life; Perfect and Blessed.

In this remembrance of ourselves we have the means to bring peace to every thought and harmony to every conflict. See the world in the "Light of Love".

I invite you to visit my website and download your Bonus copy of the workbook "Perceptions". This insightful, artistic and vibrantly activating adjunct to *Navigating The Winds of Change* presents the opportunity for you to embark on a journey of discovery that opens the door to expanding your awareness to the beauty of life and embracement of your true nature.

stevenmanatrink.com

Day Fourteen

Epigenetics / DNA

It is important for us to understand the role of Epigenetics and how it plays in our version of *This Is Your life*. When we become aware of something that enriches the quality of our lives, the only excuse for avoiding applying it in our everyday existence is our relationship with the devotion and love of self.

One thing scientists may pay little attention to but that I find important is the primary function of the body in reference to the DNA: to alert us when we are out of alignment with creative consciousness. If we take the time and become aware of the signals, our bodies will tell us when we are disconnected from the universal energy of love.

Groundbreaking research in cell biology and quantum physics pioneered by cellular biologist Bruce Lipton, Ph.D., shows that our DNA is influenced by signals from outside the cell membrane, changing the way diseases are observed, cured and most important, prevented. The science brings new insights to an exploding medical arena of *Energy Medicine* and is known as the Science of Epigenetics.

We live in an energetic universe composed of frequencies and vibrations. Our beliefs, perceptions, the food we eat, the air we breathe, the words we speak and the ecological systems in which we live, translates into a vibrational frequency that carries information and is broadcasted to our cells. Neuroscience has established that our conscious mind and subconscious programming are epigenetic influences, in the form of vibrational signals that alter the energy fields of our cells and shape the expression of our DNA. The frequency signals generated have a profound effect on our vitality and well-being. The informational signals are picked up by the receptors of our cell membranes and passed on to our DNA, influencing the expression and the functional instructions that are communicated to the cells of our body.

"Epi" implies influencing traits originating from above, in addition to, or on top of genetics through the cell membrane. "Genetics" pertains to the DNA in the nucleus, the library of blueprints, which is found inside of each living organism or individual cell. The vibrational frequencies of the epigenetic factors have zero effect on the actual sequence or structure of the DNA. However, they do reflect back to the quality of the life we are experiencing since they influence the functional information that the DNA expresses or communicates to our cells. Therefore, Epigenetics relates to the vibrational influences that effect the expression of DNA from above or outside the gene.

The fundamentals of the Science of Epigenetics lie in tracing the signal outside the cell back to its origins. The science looks for the energy flow that causes the DNA blueprint to activate a particular pattern, the driving force behind the way it expresses itself. The research discovered that our genes communicate their instructional information to the cells of our bodies according to the frequencies generated by our feelings, beliefs, emotions, and thoughts as well as the influences of our external environment. Similar to the keys of a piano, the sequences that you press gives rise to the sound or tune you create. In this way, a tune carries with it a specific energy imprint and vibration. When gratitude and appreciation are felt, our DNA responds by relaxing, the strands unwind, and the length of the DNA strands lengthens. When the denser, low frequency of anger, fear, frustration, or stress is expressed, the DNA responds by tightening up, and the strands become shorter, inhibiting our connection to the higher levels of living. Doctors and researchers are enthusiastic about this life-changing discovery and are now looking towards the energy frequencies that cause the DNA to express itself, in order to promote optimum health and cure diseases.

René Descartes, the French philosopher, whose famous statement was, "I think, therefore I am," was actually assuming that our thoughts, attitudes, personalities, and, specifically, our minds are separate and have zero influence over our bodies. When we look at his statement today, we realize that Descartes had his belief backward. It is now widely accepted that the body and mind are fully integrated. Science has recognized that our mental state has measurable physical influences on our entire being, down to the very essence of our DNA.

Fear is the emotion that the act of change awakens in us. It is based on an illusionary story conceived by the ego-mind and questions reality. However, fear can be our greatest friend. It beckons us to explore and discover what is true in the plays that are unfolding as the stories of our lives.

The body is the instrument panel that alerts us to physical malfunctions and lets us know that it is time to review our values and check our connection to our wisdom and inner truth. The illusionary dramas and fears of loss that the ego-mind weaves and our attachment to the outcome that we find to be familiar and secure cause disease to our physical form. Remember, almost all physical illness stems from the separation from love and the loss of self.

Our performance in the theater of life, when rooted in the embodiment of wisdom and truth, is a reflection of our thoughts and vibrational energy patterns that are of high density. Therefore, the informational signals we project onto any moment or situation sets into motion what blueprints will be selected and read by our DNA and passed on as functional instructions to our cells. From there, our bodies and our realities follow suit according to the instructions set forth from our focus and the vibrational energy within it.

Research has also confirmed that future generations, through cellular inheritance, can experience those same vibrational influences. Therefore, in every perception lies a potential of great significance. All that is required to be the star in the stories we have written for ourselves is to focus utterly and completely in the perception of how we would like to experience our lives in the reality of trust and Oneness. Perception is the ticket to our academy award celebration.

Every emotion, including hate, anger, resentment, or fear, originates as a story from the mind. All feelings of joy, trust, passion, or beauty fall under the umbrella of love and emanate from the heart. Both emotions and feelings emit a specific vibrational frequency that influences our DNA, contributing to disease or well-being.

Stress bathes our cells in adrenalin, cortisol, and other hormones that are all directly responsible for up to 90 percent of our illnesses, impairing the health of our bodies and our performance in the stories of our lives. Love bathes our cells in dopamine and oxytocin, considered to be the happy hormones that are responsible for our vitality and well-being. Our response to the environment around us has the potential to either surround our cell membranes in fear-based or crisis messages that transmit low-density energy or high-frequency nurturing/loving vibrations that support our radiance and spirits.

Epigenetic Science strongly upholds the belief that our world of perception is unreal, always changing and based on interpretation. It is in this land of illusion that we judge and view ourselves in relationship to our experiences. Perception is a major factor that influences our DNA expression and calls for a complete re-evaluation of life. It is a function of the body and therefore represents a limit on awareness to what is real. Our perceptions, based on our interpretation of what's happening, immerse our cells in certain frequencies that have an effect on our morphogenetic energy field that surround each of our cells.

What is *Real* always was and always is, and will always be. It is changeless throughout eternity. However, in our world of time, of change, of beginnings and endings, when we look through the eyes of the heart we will find there is only love. It is permanent, eternal, and finite. It sometimes can be difficult to recognize, but it is always present. Love applies to everything that the Universe created and only what was created in love is real. It is the most nourishing of all vibrations, the highlight of our story and the expression of our DNA.

The research makes it possible for us to see that just because we are genetically programmed a certain way, we also have the power to make choices that change that the expression of the genetic program. What we are thinking, feeling and believing is changing the genetic expression and chemical composition of our body on a moment-by-moment basis. When we understand that with every feeling and thought, in every instant, we are performing epigenetic engineering on our own cells, we suddenly have a degree of leverage over our health and happiness that makes all the difference.

Meeting Dr. Bruce Lipton was a divine intervention. Laura and I made arrangements, spontaneously, to attend his workshop in San Francisco after becoming aware of his program. In the rush to get us to the workshop, for we had to leave the next morning, I was informed when arriving at the airport for our departure that I had booked a flight for the wrong day. However, everything was in divine order and we were able to change our flights to arrive just in time as the presentation started. The universe always delivers what is supposed to be. The information and knowledge that was brought forth by Dr. Lipton pointed my focus in a new direction and supported my devotion to enriching and living a healthier and more loving life. I remain in gratitude for this life shifting experience.

> The root cause for essentially all physical health conditions is linked to our perceptions and their related effects on our energy fields.

If our civilization and planet are to flourish in the times to come, then it is imperative that we start to take conscious action from a new perspective other than the one that created the problems at hand. It is impossible to solve our difficulties by only using the mind, the master of questions, stories, and the creator of duality—the source of human suffering.

To live in the fullness of life, in the alignment of harmony and balance, we must first need to fine tune the epigenetic signals or frequencies stemming from the out of tune, sabotaging and limiting beliefs harbored in our subconscious mind. Once we become aware that these invisible programs are running our life, for the mind is limited by what it believes, we can employ the tool of Transpersonal Hypnosis to tune–up the instrument that creates the harmonics emanating from within. The next step in the dance of life is one that we can take based on this awareness and our *devotion* to a new way of living.

Tap in to the music that plays from your Heart. Listen to the songs of your guiding intuition. The symphony of life is the music of eternity and dancing to the beat that embraces love is our destiny.

True reality is simply the embracing of the experience and feeling of love. It is the only constant in our ever-changing world of perceptions.

~~ The joys in our life show us that love is the only reality ~~

Reflections

Inspirations Ignited by the Soul

"I am in alignment with the pulse of life and
awakened to the recognition of all that I am"

Our responsibility to our health and vibrancy lies in the awareness of how our body reflects the choices and actions we take in relationship to self-love. The more we choose to embrace life from a place that brings Liberation and Joy, the more profound effect it will have on how our DNA feeds and nurtures our cells with the information they "Love" to receive. We are fully responsible for our vibrational state of Being in any given moment.

When we are balanced and Heart-Focused, our life experiences reflect it. Taking conscious command of the moment as it presents itself is the strongest possible response we can make, regardless of the nature of the circumstances. Know that we are able to choose to step back, at will, from the heat of the moment and make the conscious choice to shift our energy to one emanating from the place of Heart centeredness.

The time has come to pay more attention to our state of being which directly influences our state of health. We are experiencing a massive shift in our lifestyle that is having profound effects on our well-being. It is in our best interests to apply the wisdoms that you have been divinely introduced to into your consciousness and take action from a higher perspective. We need to do the work if we want to live in harmony, balance and celebration.

Day Fifteen

Awakening of Self

I have found that over the years of experiencing the mountains and valleys of life that we needed first to give ourselves permission to allow our minds to focus on what is beautiful and loving. I have learned that if I hold this vision, it calls forth the birthing of more joy, harmony, and love.

Love is abundant in all of nature's creations—the magnificent sunset painted on the canvas of a distant sky, the melodic song of the sparrow welcoming spring, the touch of a warm wind gently caressing our skin, or the wonderful sweet fragrance of a blossoming red rose. This is the real world—a world created from love. In this world, everything is happening for us. It raises our awareness to the Oneness and to the witnessing of the beauty of creation in all.

The truth that arises from the heart is the essence of purity and completeness. It carries the all truthfulness and organic beginning of creation and flows freely into eternity. It is the only truth that exists. It is the truth that will always remain the same. It is eternal, forever, and always.

> *Truth is beyond understanding, it can only be known.*

In the world of man's mind-made reality, the perception of what is happening is one of happening *to you* in contrast to *for you*. It is observed through the eyes of ego-mind. In this illusionary world, our perception of what's happening is based on the past and the projection into the future of a story our ego-mind has created. Either way, in this world of blame and fear, we are portrayed as the victims of circumstances and are powerless.

In consciously directing my awareness to my thoughts, I have been choosing to view the world through the lens of the heart-mind that guides me onto a path of harmony when faced with struggle. Conflict usually arises when there is a pull between the mind and the heart. We tend to wander off course, separating from the Oneness when we forget our organic truth and begin to identify ourselves by our minds' fictitious stories and the illusions that depict us as less than who we really are. Therefore, I need to continually remind myself to ask questions and explore *who I am* from the perspective of the conscious intelligence that created our existence.

Our journeys are an exercise in embracing the truth from our own recognized personal experience of it and simply being completely present in that experience.

In our quest for self-realization, we become aware of a source of *knowingness* as the nature of our truth; while at the same time experiencing being present in Oneness within the world of the duality of linear and abstract perception. As we continue to stay alert to the ego-mind's tricks of deception, we open doorways and cross thresholds that connect us to other levels of our *Being* and expressions of our divine nature. It is from this experiential groundwork that we are able to be a frame of reference to others who are also in the process of embracing their true nature in the experience of humanness. In this way, we pave an energetic path for them to follow in their divine journeys.

Discovering the qualities of our essences, which are aspects of our divine identity, allows us to experience Oneness in the fullness of the experience. Oneness is more than an aspect of self. It is pure awareness. We are a total reflection of the vibrational frequency of love consciousness expressed within the context of physical form.

It takes very little effort to be who we are. The spiritual practices in which we engage sets the stage for the experience to take place on its own. Our choice is always available in every ongoing moment to embody our knowingness of our divine nature. It has to do with simply being completely present in the experience of it.

Love is all that is … which includes all that we are.

To shift the circumstances we have encountered in the journeys of our lives, it is necessary to focus upon our state of *Being* rather than the conditions themselves. We understand these concepts in theory, but now we are being asked, as well as given the opportunity, to shift our focus away from the details of the illusions of the material world and trust the process of divine guidance as we put what we understand into practice. Our challenge, at this point, is to watch the logical mind as it attempts to interfere and lure us into the deception of other possibilities. It is in our focus of awareness that will enable us to nourish our state of *Being* and feel the richness of our experience of Oneness.

When we have a readiness to surrender our fears of letting go to our perceptions of self as our ego-mind's linear identity and embrace ourselves to be in Oneness with our own states of divine presence, then we get to experience what is known as enlightenment.

Spiritual awakening is an ongoing process that brings us to a new level of recognition in our awareness and perception. It is a shift in our inner vibrational frequency and puts us in conscious alignment with who we truly are. I am truly grateful for the life lessons the soul seeks for its growth. In this new perception of the real world, I have found my loving self: pure joy, pure love.

~~ Our ability to experience the physical embracement of love is a gift the soul gives itself ~~

Reflections

Inspirations Ignited by the Soul

"I choose to feel in perfect peace.
It is from this perception that my world arises."

How we are experiencing our situation in the moment is the reflection of our perception.

As we come from a place of trust, harmony and peace we invite into our life the experiences that reflect our most inner vibration. Be consciously aware and start looking at every situation from a "Higher" perspective, a spiritual reality, other than from a play-by-play viewpoint. Remember, in all cases the universe always sets us up to succeed. When we trust in the universe and seek the truth from within we will be uplifted and be shown that our external life is but a dream.

Spend this day in perfect peace and you will certainly experience only joy as the outcome.

Day Sixteen

Energy of Consciousness

The universal law of vibration was a revealing discovery I had embraced early in my spiritual adventures. It shifted my perception of navigating the currents that change brings forth. It is one of the foremost cosmic laws, which states: "Nothing rests, everything moves, everything vibrates." The acceptance and understanding of the law of frequency became the very platform that would provide the basis for my spiritual growth.

Quantum physics tells us that everything is actually in a constant state of motion. Albert Einstein discovered $E=MC2$ and proved to the scientific community that atoms and subatomic particles are vibrating frequencies of pure energy that give them the appearance of being solid. Science and spirituality are now in alignment, both confirming that we live in an illusionary world.

"Life is frequency"

Energy is the fabric of the universe. All matter originates from energy. It is the vehicle that carries the consciousness of creation. It is information in the form of vibrational frequencies. All thoughts, beliefs, prayers, and intentions are also in the form of vibrational frequencies that influence multiple potentials to outcomes. Everything is energy vibrating and is influenced by it.

As a part of energy in consciousness, human thought forms are some of the most influential of all energies in our universe. Compassion, forgiveness, love, and trust are powerful, high frequency energies that are profoundly empowering and motivating. They are associated with universal consciousness.

To continue to thrive and stay rooted in that higher energy field takes awareness of our disconnection from it. Separation becomes apparent when we experience striving, struggle, conflict, pain, and suffering. All emotions are mind-made and stem from the ego's perspective of self. They carry a low-density vibrational frequency that compromises harmony, balance, and celebration.

It's in observing our thoughts we begin the process of change.

In his book *The Art of Happiness*, the Dali Lama stated, "Before you can change anything in your life, you first have to be aware of what it is you want to change." It is our responsibility and our devotion to ourselves to live in the awareness of having the opportunity to *choose* the direction of focus when thoughts arise, to select the actions we take, and to live our lives from the integrity of our innate wisdom. The very intent of our existence on this dimensional plane that we describe as our reality is to live in a world of harmony and balance and to physically experience the embodiment of love. There is zero separation between thought and what we are living. As we become more familiar working with energy frequencies, it becomes easier to give ourselves permission to align with the higher frequency of universal consciousness rather than the low-density frequency of illusions.

What we think, what we feel, and what we manifest is always in vibrational alignment.

As I began choosing to observe my experiences from the perspective of frequency, I realized that there was one factor that remained constant: the sense of Oneness with all that surrounds us. This is the potential in which we have been gifted. It is the opportunity to create the heart's desire simply by our own awareness to the choices between the intellectual advice of the mind and ego or the loving guidance of the heart. This is where the joy of being alive is felt in its full expression and becomes part of all life that is universally visible. At the subatomic level, we find the universal spirit that expresses itself through our physical minds and bodies. This energy-consciousness is present in all of life's creations.

Consciousness is the space that houses the wisdoms and truths of creative intelligence, permeating and encompassing all of life. It provides the background matrix for the architecture of our DNA. It is the predominant binding force for the whole universe. When we take away the ego-mind's perspective of who we *think* ourselves to be, what is left is consciousness.

Albert Einstein, Nikola Tesla, and the science of quantum physics have shown us that the fabric of the universe is composed of vibrational strings expressed as energy. Every single cell and organ system, as well as the entire physical body, is encompassed and surrounded by its own individual energy field. The basis of every state of mind and matter, including conditions of disease or health, is their primary state of vibration. Therefore, the very life we live is a reflection of our own vibrational essence and the creative force in the unfolding stories of our lives. We have the opportunity to observe each thought through the eyes of the storytelling ego-mind or from the love and empowerment of the heart. It is these individual choices, based on our degree of consciousness, that plays a role and influences the expression of our DNA and, consequently, our health and well–being.

The billions of cells that comprise our bodies are orchestrating together for the benefit of our physical forms. This information empowers us to consciously influence every biochemical event, through the understanding of epigenetics.

The heart-centered intentions behind our choices in life are where all true healing takes place. The purification of our physical forms is the single most significant activity to focus upon at this time. The molecular changes that occur in our bodies are triggered energetically as a result of frequency changes at a mass consciousness level and by our individual and personal choices. Trusting our inner guidance as our own truth, even if this defies logic, reason, and the basic ground rules we were conditioned to believe as true, will raise our level of vibrational frequency, creating the epigenetic influences that will result in vibrant well-being.

Our work is easy: to be in the awareness of the present moment and allow our heart-centered connectedness to be the inner guide. Welcome the information that surfaces from the depths of our cells and treat it with love, compassion, and the embracement of our perfection. Our world as we embark upon it now is filled with higher consciousness and vibrational frequencies supporting our greatest outcome. It took observation and practice before I became acclimated with the new levels of vibrations and the techniques for harnessing my awareness of the shifting energies as they occurred in my daily life.

Love is the encompassing essence of life in all of creation. It is the highest vibration and what we have come here to experience, embrace, and embody in full consciousness. This is our life's mission, our purpose, and the underlying reason we have chosen to experience ourselves in physical form. All else is an illusion. Only love exists.

Embodying love is more than a mental process. It is a surrendering of heart and soul and the relinquishing of all the trappings of identity. It is the essence of love itself that radiates from within the divine core of every expression of life. The embracement of self-love allows us to experience the undeniable sense of inner peace and the beautiful feeling of bliss.

Love is who and what we are.

To realize the full potential of my journey, it was necessary for me to abandon the struggle toward finding the illusive peace that I have been searching for. Surrendering my fear of the darkness and giving up any need to direct or control the outcome became my intention. Knowing that I am part of the universal hologram and that I am being guided to navigate the currents of life from a higher perspective allowed me to glide on the divine, uplifted by the winds of change.

Consciousness is a highly intelligent force and the most powerful influencer of energy in the universe. It emanates from the intelligence of creation. A higher consciousness allows us a choice between living in an environment of war or peace.

War is perceived through the intellect and complexity of the mind; peace through the simplicity and eyes of the heart. In recent times, Mother Theresa, Mahatma Gandhi, and Nelson Mandela embodied these higher frequencies.

The enhancement of our inner vibrations, which are the point of attraction to the experiences in our lives, is key to our radiance, abundance, and joy. Therefore, the very lives we live are a reflection of our own vibrational essences. We are the creative forces in the unfolding stories of our journeys, and it's time to begin to experience life from the perspective of being the artist.

The functional world is what we currently live in, but it is only an illusion. The real world, which is unseen, lies in the wisdom of the heart, the world within, and the place where we truly dwell.

In the past, I had held on to the idea of how life is supposed to be. However, now I can see why my life events continued to reflect a perspective that indicated the effect of circumstances beyond my control. When I became aware that I was still looking for answers outside of my own inner guidance, I was then able to direct my focus inward. Consequently, the times when my deepest doubts and fears surfaced became less and less prevalent. Eventually, I made the transition from *believing* to *knowing* to *embodying* a truth that was always present.

At the point when my frequency became more stable at the higher stages, I began to experience a new level of conscious awareness and understanding that came from beyond the mind. At higher levels of vibration, our perceptions take on an abstract quality that is challenging to justify by the linear logic of mind. What we think, feel, believe, and speak is what we will create as our experiences. This includes our life circumstances and the health of our physical bodies.

Over the years, I have finally come to realize that there were, at all times, basically only two choices I could make: *unloving* or *loving*. To be conscious that I have a choice between unloving and loving became my point of focus in every thought, action, and experience that I encountered. It was a blessing—the gift of a lifetime—to be given this insight. It allowed me to energetically detach from my stories, so I could live in the present moment of harmony, balance, and joy. Reality, for me, now took on a new face.

Consciousness + Devotion = Divine Expression

Reflections

Inspirations Ignited by the Soul

"My Heart is at peace and filled with Joy, my spirit is eternally free".

The mind is always busy figuring things out, analyzing, deducting, conceptualizing or worrying. It keeps us distracted from the very thing that brings peace, harmony and balance: the silence between our thoughts.

In the "Light" of the Heart we discover our Truth. That is why the ego-mind is so afraid of us embracing our sacred home. The ego-mind knows that it can only exist in the "darkness" of the mind and looks at Love as its' sole enemy.

"Does It really matter in the scope and purpose of life." This is what we need to ask ourselves. It is a mantra that we can bring into our consciousness whenever faced with the challenges of everyday living. It shifts our values and puts all things in perspective.

Releasing your mind to the embrace of trust, is allowing Spirit to flow easily and effortlessly into every cell of your body. Spirit is the energy of life and is eternally free.

Day Seventeen

Facing Fear / Trusting Life

What road are we choosing to take, facing fear or trusting life? Most people I have come in contact with would choose to face fear. It is something they have been living with all their lives. We have been conditioned from the time we were born to defend or protect ourselves from life's unknowns. We have been told that it is intelligent to question and doubt as opposed to trust. We have fears of sickness, death, poverty, and even love. Our own inner scripts, which reside in our subconscious minds, are the unique combination of these fears, attitudes, and messages that we believe are the truth.

The subconscious mind lacks knowing the difference between truth and fiction, reality and fantasy, or right and wrong. Our beliefs are just knowns that constantly change and define the way we perceive our world and ourselves. We have learned them consciously and unconsciously through our experiences and the words and actions of significant people in our lives. Thus, fear is something that is quite familiar and comfortable to us. The interesting thing is that we were born with only two basic fears: the fear of falling and the fear of loud noises; all others are learned. At all times, we are either expressing love, which is a feeling, or expressing fear, which is an emotion. Simply put, one feels good.

Fear comes from our basic lack of trust and the result of negative perception. It is an illusion created by the mind and our disconnection from the presence of the light (love and joy). When we are connected to our higher consciousness, there is zero fear, anxiety or insecurity about the future. However, the ego-mind will always intervene and try to pull you away from truly connecting to where trust lives, for it fears its life and can only exist in the absence of trust. When we take time and allow ourselves to go within and trust our deepest wisdom, all fear dissolves in the light of love's embrace.

Trust allows you to dance with the energies of life.

Every experience we encounter simply offers us an opportunity to grow and change. It will ask us if we are willing to let go, if we are willing to trust, and if we are willing to be in the present moment. The path we choose that will lead to our liberation must be traveled blindly. Trust is the only vehicle that will take us from the point of living with fear to the point of living in the experience of peace, harmony, and liberation. We are asked with each experience to surrender the fear to the universe and trust the divinity of the process.

Understand that trust is beyond mental ideas or something that is right or wrong, good or bad. By trusting, we are giving complete acceptance and confidence over to the universe to provide us with everything we need, at the time we need it, outside of the times when the ego-mind wants it in order to feel safe or secure. Fear and negativity are absent in the presence of trust. It is necessary to embrace trust in order to feel free and live in the moment, to experience our true essence. However, even with embodying trust, we will still experience life's mountains and valleys.

Accept the fact that fear will always pop its head into our lives. It plays an integral part in creating the duality that exists on this planet. It sets up the opportunity to choose to move beyond it and to ascend into the realm of trust.

Our resistance to change, that at one time was anticipated, is now absent under the umbrella of trust. The fears, doubts, and feelings of reluctance are replaced with the openness to experience a new way of perceiving the world and our places within it.

Whatever fears and resistance we may be experiencing, acknowledge and surrender them to the universe. Every little shred of guilt, anger, hurt, and pity should be given over to the *light*. All emotions of worry, doubt, confusion, and anxiety dissipate in the love of the *light*. Trying to hold on to what it is that we think we need out of fear of losing it is the root of all human suffering.

Life gives us constant opportunities to practice spiritual trust and to surrender our egos with their illusionary stories to a higher consciousness. Discover the gifts, possibilities, and miracles that are waiting on the other side of our fears. Let awareness work. Simply be aware of the fear and feel it fully, and then illuminate the darkness with the light of your consciousness. Give yourself permission to let go and surrender to trust, knowing that divine guidance is always with you. The movement takes place of itself.

Trust is beyond logic and belief.

When we focus beyond the illusionary creations of the mind to our deepest wisdom, we truly connect to what we can trust. Our whole process on this planet is learning to trust in the divine process and to bring our awareness to the voice within. It is our birthright to live in joy. It is our birthright to be the fullest expression of all that is.

~~ When our reality is rooted in illusion, it was
created from a fear-based perception ~~

Reflections

Inspirations Ignited by the Soul

"Every loving thought I have is true; all others are a cry for love"

Our mind and thoughts belong to us alone. The power to shift or exchange each illusionary fear based thought for one of Harmony, Peace or Trust lies in the gift of Awareness and the perceived value we bestow upon ourselves.

In our perceived world that we live in merely reflects our internal frame of reference; our dominant ideas, wishes, feelings and emotions. Fear itself is an appeal for help, a call for Love, attempts to master the fear is useless. True resolution rests entirely on mastery through Love. In Love where Truth resides there is nothing to fear.

Devote your attention and focus to the point of observing your mind at all times. Become conscious of your corresponding feelings or emotions. Feelings come from your Heart Mind, emotions your ego-mind. One feels pleasurable, the other a cry for Love.

Live each moment in the Heart of Consciousness.

I invite you to visit my website to receive your Free download *Gift* of the workbook "Perceptions". This insightful, artistic and vibrantly activating adjunct to *Navigating The Winds of Change* presents the opportunity for you to embark on a journey of discovery that opens the door to expanding your awareness to the beauty of life and embracement of your true nature.

stevenmanatrink.com

Day Eighteen

Conscious Creation

The planet is under what I term reconstruction. We are riding on the crest of change in the evolution of the consciousness of humankind. We are at the threshold of a new way of experiencing life, where integrity, transparency, and love are the building blocks for the new structure of existence. Individually, we play an integral role toward birthing a more loving world. The illusions and beliefs that we perceived through the lenses of the ego–mind are falling away as we open our eyes to the new world where we are nourished by the reality of our divine essence.

When we look around at the lives of other individuals or at the fearful world we live in, it is easy to formulate the question: What has happened to the freedom and celebration that life is supposed to grant us? We are experiencing the opposite of what we seek because most of our world still lives attached to the stories and illusions created by the ego-mind's intention to separate us from our birthright of living in joy and truth.

Our journeys, which are centered in a state of *Being* take on an entirely new perspective as we come to understand life as a wavering road that unfolds into one's heart desire and the joyousness of creation.

The actions we take are in response to perceived reality, seeded from our perceptions, in the experience of what is happening. We are influenced by our focus on either the illusions of the mind-made stories or on the gentle whispering of the eternal wisdom and truth emanating from our hearts.

> Our state of self-awareness defines
> what is perceived as one's life.

The attention we put on our own blossoming consciousness and the application of heart wisdom to every thought, word, and interaction with others and ourselves is our daily task.

The joys experienced in the adventures that life *gifts* us would be absent if everything in our lives was just comfortable, remained the same, or was predictable. We would be living in a stagnant world, void of the changes that gives us insight, perspective, and the guideposts to the portal of a new reality and the liberation we seek. Ultimately, all changes lead to an internal shift that allows us to reconstruct the stories of our lives in a way that aligns with our hearts' truest desires.

Our understanding that growth requires change allows us to give ourselves permission to accept the experience as something that is happening *for* us instead of *to* us. However, understanding is only half of the equation.

Surrender to the will of the wind. It will elevate us to new heights and to the exalted experience of feeling alive; it will take us home.

The first and essential step to begin intentionally and consistently creating the quality of life that harmonizes with our heartfelt yearnings requires a simple and conscious choice of accepting responsibility for the circumstances that we are presented with. It is profoundly transformational and will enable us to have a conscious influence on the outcomes experienced in each and every area of our lives.

A new chapter is beginning as we view life differently. Our understanding now is to satisfy the heart's desire, reaching fulfillment and experiencing joy as our birthright.

We are transcending from a world that reflects the strategies of the mind, the mentality of competition, and the world of material entrapment into a global consciousness that embraces the unity of Oneness. This is a state of elevated awareness—a state that most of us only get a glimpse of from time to time, where sensibilities are heightened, the heart center is open, and we are attuned to a level of focus and wisdom that goes beyond habitual experience. This is where we continually make more loving and nurturing choices. Living by conscious creation becomes a new way of life. Our life experiences begin to reflect the dynamics of our choices. We begin to make selective and conscious choices as to where and with whom we continue to interact and associate. Ultimately, we choose to step back from any disharmony and tune in to our own inner compasses, guiding us to individuals and situations that foster the ultimate experience of joy.

> Liberation from the attachment of
> outcome is more than a concept;
> it is our ultimate goal toward which we are heading.

The level of harmony or struggle we manifest in our life experiences measures the degree to which we attain our sense of freedom. We are on the threshold of experiencing life from a higher vibration of awareness, and it is leading us to the liberation we have been seeking.

The playing field of our world has changed; however, the basic universal laws by which it is governed will always remain etched into eternity. The hints of joy that have come our way have most likely been acquired by default, in the absence of consciousness, rather than by the *wisdom* of knowing that we have a choice. It is our ability to move with grace through the uncertainty of life that is the sign of mastering the universal laws. This is the skill that I am cultivating within myself and I encourage you to cultivate within yours. The paths that we now choose to take in this new paradigm will be made from a conscious intent rather than from decisions that are rooted in the ego-mind, old habits, or fears. Trusting in the divinity of the experience and allowing life to unfold into its perfection becomes the focus of our attention. The absence of the tendency to try to force a result through mind-directed effort is ultimate liberation.

-- Our very lives are a testimonial to change --

Reflections

Inspirations Ignited by the Soul

"In this moment, I choose to see a world of beauty and allow all my experiences to be joyous and loving"

We can change our attitude towards something very quickly. This gives us the power over our perceived world. In a matter of moments our experience can be entirely different than what it was prior to the world we lived in a few moments ago.

It is in the way we choose to respond to an encounter, from the perspective of our self-love that makes the difference in how we experience the situation. Looking through the lenses of the Heart allows us to move forward in Harmony, rather than a negative experience.

Recall a situation that was frustrating, an individual who became annoying or any encounter that put you in a bad mood. What different approach in your attitude could you have chosen in order to experience harmony in that situation?

The key is to be aware of your attitude; it belongs to you.

Day Nineteen

Language Sculpting

Frequency plays an integral part in our well-being; therefore, we have to pay attention to how we formulate our thoughts and speech, which are both vibrational energies. The world is the stage that allows us to play out the script that we had written for ourselves before we were born upon this planet of duality. Our part is simply to remember our true nature from the perspective of the bigger picture.

While visiting the Big Island of Hawaii early in my relationship with Laura, I was introduced to a very conscious and remarkable woman who brought a new perspective and awareness to the way I was to forever formulate my thoughts and communicate to others. Star Newman taught me how our language, the spoken word, carries a vibrational frequency that can change our neurological pathways. She kept tutoring me with every sentence I uttered, constantly pointing out how my words and their corresponding vibrational frequencies were undermining my quest for joy. I finally realized, after continually being shown, that I was blind to the fact that the sentences and language I was using were compromised by my common usage of words and the conditioning by the society and culture in which I was living. I was devoted to being at my fullest potential. Putting my ego to the side, I surrendered and allowed Star to direct my attention to the way I spoke and then to language sculpt my sentences and words to their highest and most uplifting vibration.

One of the most impressive discoveries in the science of epigenetics is that our thoughts as well as the spoken word can have an influencing effect on how our DNA instructs information to our cells, directly affecting our health, vibrancy, and state of well-being. Therefore, it is entirely natural for our DNA to react to language. The very concept of our DNA being influenced by words is premised on the understanding that the fabric of the universe is vibration, and words carry with them the frequency of intention.

It is remarkable that our own DNA expression—influenced by the vibrational frequencies of our emotions and feelings, all of which are expressed in language and words—controls how the body experiences disease or a vibrant and healthy life. We can simply be reprogrammed by human speech. How easy and beautiful is that?

This information helped me understand that we are all part of and connected to the whole, and the way I express myself has the power to alter my genetic and DNA expression moment by moment. When I started to monitor, with conscious awareness, the words and vibrational energy I brought to any situation, I started to make the highest possible contribution to the well-being of all.

We use words to describe the thoughts, emotions, opinions, and beliefs that are stored in our conscious minds. However, our subconscious minds store everything as images. There are zero words to record those views. Yet, we are still able to express them in the language of words.

Every word we speak generates specific neurochemicals in our brains that flow through our pathways, directing energy, thoughts, and creating experiences according to the pictures and perceptions that are associated with the words. Our DNA receptors read the environmental energy field in terms of frequencies and respond accordingly by communicating instructional behavioral functions to our cells.

> *How we think and what we say, as well as our actions, determines how we perceive our experiences of life.*

We have the capability to shift things in the moment by simply being conscious that we have a choice to be proactive. Our choice involves the ability and willingness to sculpt our words and sentences to a vibrational frequency that is aligned with heart consciousness. This especially applies to the words we speak to ourselves.

The realization that our vibrational state of mind can be shifted, changed, or transmuted through the application of words increases the power behind our intentions. This takes place when we become aware of the creative nature of vibrational frequencies and the principles of language and word sculpting.

Speaking from the heart creates a direct high-frequency path that bypasses the ego-mind and goes directly into our conscious behavior. As we shift our inner and outer dialogue, we are actually changing our physiology. We are in alignment with the harmony of our bodies. It can be shown by kinesiology or muscle testing of the sculptured words that the new communication is stronger.

Language sculpting trains us to be mindful about every word. It prompts us to be more consciously aware. We feel uplifted as sculpting is applied. We become easy to understand in our communication. When we are easy to understand, we get along better with the world. Consider that 90 percent of poor relationships or wars between individuals or nations are due to poor communication. It is an art form that uses words and language to create beautiful new realities. Language sculpting is a living technology, as it can change the direction of our lives in a moment and propel us to new insights while directly altering the neurological pathways in our brains.

By consciously choosing the most powerful words with the highest uplifting frequencies, we allow the energy of the language to be expressed into our lives in the form of harmony, balance, and well-being. Our experiences will be reflected in joy and enrichment.

> Our devotion is rooted in the embracement of the divinity within our own hearts.

Virtually all communications are delivered in common usage, which defines how language is commonly used. It is usually thought, spoken, or written in a certain way. Common usage is how our culture and media communicate. It is how our parents, schools, and all social structures converse, how books are written and films are scripted. An example of the typical way that common usage language is used in our society can be found in our government's Department of War. It is a matrix of thinking that is skewed in a certain way. Aside from *war* a very low vibrational frequency word, it is the opposite of the intention of harmony and conflicting to its purpose. The wording sends mixed messages. It would be more appropriate and beneficial to apply conscious usage and rename it the Department of Peace.

Negative words are low-density frequencies. If we are using common usage expressions associated with fear, lack, or uncertainty or words that close off the attraction of abundance, based on the law of attraction, we will invite experiences into our lives reflective of the frequencies we are sending out. Parents, for instance, are fond of saying things like, "Have fun, and don't get hurt." This creates two different thought forms and confusion. It is also overlaid with the sense of anxiety. Its best to communicate one clear picture with conscious usage words: "Have fun, and be careful."

It is best to learn to pay attention to our thoughts, and then word sculpt negative, confusing, or common usage vocabulary with *conscious* usage language. It encourages harmonious behaviors and positive responses in others. Language sculpting also transforms our lives into those of fulfillment and gratitude. We must start to choose the words that manifest the intentions of our communication. It is a skill that can be learned and improved with practice.

COMMON USAGE	CONSCIOUS USAGE
Don't mess up.	Get it right.
No, not	Zero, other than
No problem.	It is my pleasure.
If you don't mind.	If it works.
Not a bad deal.	It is a good deal.
Don't make me.	I would prefer.
Not bad	Great, perfect
I am not helpless.	I am powerful.
I will not wait.	I am going.
I do not know.	I am yet to solve that.
It does not mean anything.	Show me the connection.
It is impossible.	I am sure the answer exists.
No one can fail.	Everyone will pass.

Be watchful to sculpt common usage language by eliminating words that close the door to possibilities and are low vibrational. Sentences that normally contain the words *no, can't, shouldn't, isn't, doesn't, but, don't, never, won't, not, wouldn't,* and *couldn't* can be restructured and presented in more positive, clear, and supportive way that promotes a frequency that will enhance your well-being. Each word carries its own energetic vibration and can have a profound impact on the quality of our lives. The gift of language allows us to become active creators from the moment we utter our first word.

Practicing conscious communication is the key to unlocking our full manifestation power. Thinking about what we want is only half the equation; changing our common usage language program is the missing variable.

We think, speak, and write using words, yet these seemingly neutral forms are actually the building blocks of our lives. Language is undeniably a gift. Humans are the only species to have this tool available; thus, we have a responsibility to use it consciously.

~~ There is sacredness in difficulty ~~

Reflections

Inspirations Ignited by the Soul

*"I am aware of the vibrational frequency of my thoughts, patterns
and the energy released in the form of my verbal communication"*

The thoughts and words of Joy, Peace, Beauty, Harmony, Passion,
Creativity, Inspiration, Trust, Allow and Love all evoke a feeling
associated with pleasure. Where as anger, fear, sadness, jealousy,
guilt, anxious, insecure, stress, hate, impatient and afraid all evoke
a sensation associated with pain. Every word generates specific
neuro-chemicals that flow through our system directing energy
and attracting experiences according to the emotions and feelings
that are associated with our expressions.

The task at hand is to train our mind to watch our mind, alerting
us when our thoughts and actions are other than loving. Simply,
our choices are either unloving or loving and they are based on our
self-love; the relationship with ourselves at the time.

It is necessary to continually observe our mind and to be alert to
the direction it takes us. It is easy to know which way we are headed
simply by becoming aware of how we are experiencing the situation.

Day Twenty

Trusting Divinity

I believe that most of us have experienced a view of trust that supports the illusion that everything will work out the way we would like to imagine or wish it would. It incorporates the mind's intervention into the scenario. However, when we employ the mind to bring us comfort or peace, we are allowing the storyteller to weave a fantasy that relies on a fictitious mind-made drama that we want to believe will unfold in harmony. This way of incorporating trust into our lives will, for the most part, create disappointment and despair.

It took me many times of getting knocked out of the ring to finally come to the awareness that *trust is the complete acceptance and assurance of divine intelligence.* Fear and negativity are absent in the presence of purity and the absolute nature of trust.

Our lack of trust creates fear. It is the result of disparaging perception. It is an illusion created by the ego-mind and our disconnection from the presence of love and joy. When we are in the present moment, we are connected to a higher consciousness; there is zero fear, anxiety, or insecurity about the future. However, the personality that lives in the mind—the ego that creates the contrast in life and lives off pain—will always intervene and try to pull us away from truly connecting to heart-centeredness.

> The ego's only worry is in its own death, which
> lies in our conscious choice to embrace love.

When we focus beyond the illusionary stories of the mind to our deepest wisdom, we truly connect to the divinity within us. Our whole process on this planet is learning to tune in and tap into the vibrational frequency of love—the voice calling us from the depths of our own hearts.

The life we have chosen to live simply offers an opportunity to grow, shift, and celebrate. Every experience that comes our way will ask us if we are willing to let go, if we are willing to be in the present moment, and if we are willing to trust the divinity of the process.

Trust is a major piece in the jigsaw puzzle of life. It allows us to transcend the mental constraints of the mind and cherish the very essence of our *Being*. It is the only vehicle that will transport us to a place of detachment from outcome and the expectation of results.

I learned through the events of my own life challenges and through the teachings of *A Course in Miracles* that the sole purpose of the ego-mind is to create a duality—to separate us from the experience of joy and love. My personal work was therefore to go beyond the illusionary creations of the mind, to my deepest wisdom, where I can truly connect to what it is I can trust. It became evident to me that everyone's life experience on this planet is about surrendering to and embracing trust, the universal consciousness within.

Trusting in the divinity of creation brings us to the experience of peace, harmony, abundance, and liberation. It also increases our mental acuity, puts our emotions and feelings in perspective, raises our frequency, and awakens the divine spirit that encompasses everything as Oneness. In addition, when we maintain a higher frequency, it resonates outwardly into the universe, raising the collective consciousness and the healing of our planet.

> Once the veil of fear has been lifted and our path illuminated in wisdom and truth, we encounter divine essence.

Through the observation and awareness of my experiences, I was guided to understand that fear and negativity is absent in the embracement of trust. It is necessary to trust in order to feel free and live in the moment to experience our divinity. If we want to experience the godliness of Oneness, it is necessary to manifest unity within our own beings. It is impossible to be divided within ourselves and at the same time be united unto ourselves. It's that simple.

In time, I trained my mind to alert me when I was unplugged from the consciousness of love. I developed awareness to an energy that became the point of attraction to well-being, abundance, joy, and liberation. It was a new awareness from the perspective of trust and divine order. We have chosen this reality in order to taste the experience of our own divine connectedness for the purpose of knowing the Oneness that is the very essence of who we truly are.

Living our lives from this viewpoint, where hummingbirds, dolphins, and whales reside, allows our full expression and potential to be expressed and experienced. It is a world that is based on the consciousness of nature, a place where creation unfolds into the joyousness of the moment. Living in this reality, we are aware that we have choices along the path. We follow our inner guidance systems, reflected in the awareness of the wisdom and truth within our hearts, rather than the illusionary stories of the mind.

Peace, harmony, and balance are a natural way of life. Our bodies rejoice in the alignment and nourishment of the vibrational frequency of love consciousness. Our DNA communicates health and well-being to our cells. We feel wonderful!

True healing occurs when we have succeeded in releasing the underlying low-density vibrational frequencies that have been embedded in our cellular memory for lifetimes.

Change, in itself, allows us the choice to embrace trust and experience the feelings of freedom from the attachment of outcome. However, if we are other than conscious of our choices and hold on to the drama and illusionary stories our ego-minds have woven, we live in the fear of what is yet to come rather than celebrate the joyous feeling that is only found in the moment of "now".

Does the story really matter? The bottom line is the tale that was woven by the ego-mind, being one that brings on anger, doubt, conflict, fear, sadness, resentment, jealously, or any other emotional, low-density vibrational energy is based on an illusion that we believe to be true. To try to understand the illusionary narrative so we can rationalize our emotions will do little to change anything. It's the ego's plan to divert us from connecting to the root cause of the problem and keep us in the loop of suffering.

-- All that is real is divine. --

Reflections

Inspirations Ignited by the Soul

"I embrace the place of trust and heartfelt connectedness as I move forward upon a path that supports the divinity of my unfolding story"

Trusting in the Divinity of Creation will bring us to the experience of Peace, Harmony, Abundance and Liberation. It awakens our Divine Spirit that encompasses everything as "Oneness".

Take your most serious problems and turn them over to "The Universe". Know that our Divine Essence is who we are. This puts us in contact with our eternal Wisdom, other than some external or separate force outside of ourselves. Remind yourself that absolute trust involves surrendering of all conditioning that teaches we are special or separate. The embracement of complete trust is evident in our life when what we think, feel and do are balanced and in harmony with the symphony of life.

If we want to raise our vibration in alignment with the celebration of life, then it involves the absolute trust in the Love Consciousness that created it all.

Day Twenty-One

Compassion

The starting point and basis of compassion is self-love. The embracing of our own love inspires the birth of kindheartedness. Before we can truly display compassion for others, we first have to be able to evoke it in ourselves. The compassion that resides within all of us wants to be expressed, for it is truly a manifestation of who we really are as well as a powerful healing energy.

Compassion is more than a sense of sympathy or caring for the suffering and pain of another. In order to extend true compassion, we have to take action and do whatever is required and possible to help ease or uplift the spirits of those who are suffering.

> *Compassion flows like a river from the reality of love.*

Most of the world populations are still in a state of ignorance, living in a reality that fosters illusions. Our world, at this point, is a reflection of that collective mass consciousness. Each person, in his or her own time, will awaken to the wisdom and truths of the universe. However, only when they, themselves, live the wisdom and universal truths will they be able to experience the true liberation attained from enlightenment. Know it can only take place when we are in alignment, harmony, and synchronicity with universal consciousness. It happens when it happens. When we open our hearts, it allows for the river of compassion to flow freely. The act of compassion is healing to all of creation.

Our entire human species is composed of identical human anatomy. We are all seeking to experience joy, vitality, and love and, of course, to avoid suffering. We all have an equal right to celebrate life—our birthright. It is important to realize we all are born from the same source and to love all others as we would ourselves in the Oneness of all that is.

Thinking about others with love and compassion carries a high vibration that is healing to whatever suffering and pain they may have gone through in the past, present, or what is yet to be experienced. The act of compassion, extending our love to others, frees us from our self-adoring and the grasping ego-mind. It is healing to the person who extends loving compassion and to the person to who receives that compassion. The vibration of our love goes out to the universe, bathing all creation in its frequency.

We have to be thankful and grateful to all humans and living creations that cross our paths on our sacred journeys. They inspire, evoke, and bring forth the powerful but hidden compassion of love from within our hearts. It is compassion's high vibration and healing energy that raises the collective consciousness of humankind and harmonizes with all of creation. The circumstances of others who are suffering help to develop compassion by giving us one of the greatest gifts of all: they are inviting us to develop the very quality needed most in our progress toward enlightenment.

I can relate to the experience I had as caretaker for my wife, Laura, in her last weeks of her life. I felt an enormous swelling of love and true compassion toward her. It was an experience that went beyond any other hardship that I was ever challenged with. It brought me to a new and higher level of intimacy in the facing of her death. Therefore, when we reflect on our lives at this stage of our journeys, we begin to realize that the opportunities to engage in the act of compassion are highlights in the experiences we are attracting.

Compassion is other than having pity. Pity is rooted in the ego-mind. It projects a sense of superiority and arrogance, whereas compassion flows from the heart.

> *When your ego judges someone's pain, it becomes pity; when your love touches someone's pain, it becomes compassion.*

It is easy to understand and empathize the nature of another person's pain having lived it yourself. We can only evoke compassion and reach out to another person living his dramatic story by being given a chance to experience those very same fears and emotions.

Many individuals would love to help those who are experiencing life-threatening events. However, in order to truly be of service to humanity, we have to share, give, or extend from the overflow of the abundance of the love that dwells within.

Compassion is the frequency of love. It's a blessing that nourishes our cells in the purity of love. I speak of the integrity of a vibrational frequency that is in alignment with a consciousness that manifests into the perfection of self, other than compromised by the needs of the ego, the master of disguises. Compassion leads us to find, within ourselves, the lovingness of our own true nature, for this is who and what we truly are.

~~ Compassion is the source and essence of enlightenment ~~

Reflections

Inspirations Ignited by the Soul

"With the energy of loving compassion I live in peace and harmony while embracing relationships that serve and nourish my inner truth"

We are other than a victim of our life story, but a fully responsible participant in our choices presented on our journey through life. When we choose to embrace Compassion, Gratitude, Unity and Love we raise our frequencies and awaken to the Divine Spirit that encompasses everything as "Oneness". In addition, when we maintain a higher vibration it resonates outwardly into the universe raising the collective consciousness and the healing of our planet.

By approaching all challenges from the perspective of the Heart, we serve to dissipate any low- density, epigenetic vibrational influences and transcend the fears that may inhibit us from laughing, enjoying and loving.

Please accept my offer to receive your Bonus workbook "Perceptions" that compliments *Navigating The Winds of Change*. It is available as a *Free* download on my website. The high frequency and vibrant artwork found in each chapter activates your feelings of harmony, peace and joy. The workbook is designed to awaken you in expanding your perceptions, awareness and to embracing the reality of love.

stevenmanatrink.com

Epilogue

We have arrived at this juncture at the perfect time to set our intentions on what it is we want to manifest on our journeys along the path of enlightenment. The experiences that are presented to us are directly in alignment with what we are attracting in order to cross the bridges of illusion and stand on the other side grounded in the wisdom and essence of our very beings. Our destinies wait, and all that is required is the focused intent to call forth our highest expression. The choices made will be from our level of perception, based on the conscious awareness that we now, in this moment, consider to be our reality.

I have shared with you in these writings what I have personally experienced and continue to acknowledge along my journey of Oneness. I trust that it would be enlightening, inspiring, and liberating to all who are finding themselves on the path of a new reality. My experiences, as yours, are a personalized adventure illustrating universal wisdoms, truths, and laws that were revealed to me through my adventures. I am refraining asking you to believe in my awareness's. There is skepticism and doubt in belief. However, I am strongly suggesting integrating and applying in your day-to-day life what your heart beckons you to embrace and embody. The only way to actually know the truth is to have an inner experience of it.

The wisdoms and truths—the gems gleaned from our experiences—have become our newest operating system. The illusionary world we are leaving is opening the doors to a perception of a new world. Our journeys have taken us into the depths of our experiences as we now have begun to be more consciously aware of the reality our true essence, the Oneness of divine love.

The knowledge that is acquired along the path of enlightenment liberates us from the conditioned and illusionary world we were made to believe was our reality. Being compassionate with ourselves by trusting in the divinity of the process is the consciousness we must welcome at this stage in our journeys. Like a butterfly, we too have to go through a period of metamorphosis in order to experience what we have been destined to celebrate. The movement takes place on its own, in the synchronicity and unfolding of the process. Mastery takes awareness, devotion, and continued spiritual practice. Only then can we fly, glide, and soar on the winds of change.

In loving Oneness,

Steven Mana Trink

~~ The journey is the grand adventure that is taking us back to a destination that was always our home ~~

Nightly Meditation

*"I sleep peacefully in the embrace
of the arms of the universe
and awake to the Reality of Love"*

The Wind Knows
by
Richie Niles Pollock

It's all about me
And my perceptions
What I believe
Is what I receive

Like a circle
Life is unbroken
Existence was
And will always be

The wheel must turn
The ages change
Empires rise
Just to fall again
I've got to glide
With each strong wind
That blows
Cause the wind knows

The wind knows
Which way
I need
To go

The wind knows
My destination
Has the ability
To keep on leading me
The wind knows
My destiny

It's all about me
And my awareness
Either I see or
I'm history

Finally a sign
Lights my horizon
I feel the breezes
Lifting me
I trust the wind
And just the wind
To gust me up and
Muss me
Fine tune and
Adjust me

Dust me off and
Thrust me
Where I ultimately
Must be

The wind knows
Which way
I need
To go

Knows my destination
Has the ability
To keep on
Leading me

The wind knows
My destiny
It's all about
Me

Spiritual Glossary

A

Abundance: The feeling of liberation that encompasses Trust and Joy. The sense of fulfillment that one receives when embracing the blessings of life.

Acceptance: Embracing the understanding that everything is happening according to Divine Order. Surrendering the struggle to a Higher Power.

Alignment: In harmony with the consciousness of love and the creative intelligence of the universe. Connecting to source energy, a consciousness greater than the material world.

All That Is: The creation of all existence by a Supreme Force.

Allowing: The surrendering of the dictatorship mind to the higher power of love consciousness. To trust what is yet to come.

Appreciation: The deeper connection to one's values, beliefs, meaning and purpose, which makes life worth living. When we are in a state of appreciation we are transmitting some of the highest and most spiritual energy vibrations.

Ascension: The evolutionary process of spiritual awakening that elevates you into a higher level of human consciousness.

Awakening: An evolving spiritual process of a dimension of reality, beyond the confines of the ego, that embraces your higher self or spirit giving you new definition for life. To wake up to a new reality.

Awareness: The gift of a spiritual conscious that recognizes the wisdom, truth and wholeness of our life experiences. The ability to identify the illusions created by the ego-mind and embrace the truth that lives in in the heart.

B

Beauty: A reflection of Gods creation in all of life seen from the heart of the soul. The divine origin of that beauty is within each breath.

BE: To recognize, accept and embody our divine essence in the perfection of nature's creation.

Being: Our divine spirit manifested in physical form whose highest priority is to express love, which is our core essence.

Believe: A function of the ego-mind that accepts the illusions being presented as our reality.

Birthright: Our spiritual inheritance and our God-given identity.

Blessing: An ultimate gift of love bestowed by universal or God Consciousness.

C

Celebration: The embracement, rejoicing, appreciation and gratitude of the moment. The Blessings and Miracles of Life.

Change: The process of life experiences that lead to personal transformation and the evolution of the Soul. Change is Life.

Choice: The heart-felt direction that leads us into the discovery of self-love.

Compassion: The expression and actions of love that embrace, support and nourish the Soul in all of life's' challengers.

Conflict: The pull between the mind and the heart.

Consciousness: The high vibrational and creative energy of love that permeates in all of natures creation. The awareness of the hearts guiding truths and wisdoms.

Conscious Awareness: Our focused intention to witness the experience of the moment from a higher perspective.

Conscious Intent: The focused thought of a loving act, from the perspective of heart-centeredness.

Courage: The strength to move forward in life by embracing the trust of the universe to provide and support our choices.

Core Essence: The Divine consciousness of our spiritual *being* that radiates from within. Our true nature.

Course of Miracles: The unique spiritual self-study program designed to awaken us to the truth of our Oneness with God and love. A curriculum for those seeking to achieve spiritual transformation.

Creation: The act of a universal intelligence that manifest into reality the will of God.

D

Darkness: The absence of Love

Deliberate Choices: Our conscious intentions, as seen through the eyes of the heart, to embracing love.

Detachment: The removal of expecting a specific result or outcome. The act of separating ourselves from our belief in the illusions the ego has created.

Discipline: Dedicated to moving past all the resistances which the mind creates towards achieving a goal.

Divine: The consciousness of God or a supreme force that creates all of life in perfection. Sacred or relating to God.

Divine Process: The unfolding sequence of events orchestrated by a supreme force or by which God manifests.

Divinity: The sacredness of a supreme force and the natural spiritual laws of creation. The quality of being divine. God or a divine being.

Duality: The concept and experience of life that gives us perspective of choice between living in a world of illusion or truth, separation or Oneness.

E

Ego-mind: The part of our mind that weaves stories of duality and identifies itself with the illusions that separates us from the consciousness and Oneness of creation.

Embodiment: A spiritual experience of a deep truth that you sense, feel and honor within your body.

Emotions: Low frequency energy that is manifested in our bodies that is generated by the illusionary creations of the ego-mind usually connected to stories associated with sadness, anger, jealously, doubt or fear.

Energy: The vibrational frequencies of consciousness. A Universal force that comprises the fabric of life.

Enlightenment: Self-Realization. The discovery, embracement and the embodiment of the core essence of our Being: Love

Epigenetics: The science that traces the vibrational signals from outside the cell membrane, created from our internal or external environment, that influences the expression of our DNA.

Epigenetic Influence: A vibrational frequency, originating from outside of the cell membrane that influences the expression of our DNA.

F

Feelings: The internal experience of pleasure, fulfillment or joy stemming from the heart. The awareness experienced when we are in alignment with Love.

Forgiveness: The realization of the divine law that all is in perfect order. All is in accordance of what is supposed to be. Frees oneself form holding on to an error of the mind.

Frequency: The number of energy waves that carry a specific vibration.

Fulfillment: The realization of our true self. The ultimate experience in the embodiment of Love.

Fullest Potential: The realization and the expression of our divine abilities.

G

Gem: Highly valued. A Wisdom, Insight, Knowledge or Truth.

Gratitude: The act of feeling and communicating gratefulness for the people, circumstances and material possessions in our lives. Embracing the thankfulness for the gifts bestowed by the Universe.

Growth: The shift in our consciousness to a higher perspective.

Guiding Light: The unseen path that leads us to our destination.

H

Happiness: A temporary state of delight based on what is happening in our external environment.

Harmony: To be in alignment and orchestration with universal consciousness.

Heart Centered: The core essence of consciousness that emanates wisdom and love.

Heartfelt: The experience of a loving feeling that is recognized only by our heart.

Heart Intelligence: The wisdom and truth of supreme consciousness.

Higher: The level of awareness from the perspective of a supreme power.

Higher Self: The divine core essence of our identity.

I

I AM: The name of God. Spiritual self.

Illusion: All that is perceived through the mind.

Inheritance: The rightful ownership and embracement of the celebration of love and joy in life.

Initiation: The welcoming into a new reality. Rites of passage.

Inner Guidance: Our heart-centered navigational system that embraces our innate wisdom.

Insights: Life lessons learned from our experiences. Holy moments of wisdoms.

Intention: The vibrational frequency and driving force behind our actions.

J

Journey: The path of enlightenment and self –realization.

Joy: Celebration of our Divinity.

Just Is: Zero Point, neutral. Absent of reason.

K

Knowing: Our innate awareness to truth.

Knowledge: The consciousness of God

L

Law of Attraction: Magnetic power of the universe that manifests into reality what we focus on. Like attracts like.

Law of Vibration: Basic law of the universe that states everything is energy frequency and in constant motion.

Leap of Faith: The act of taking action outside the boundaries of reason, based on complete trust that the universe will provide.

Liberation: Free from results or outcome. The experience of freedom. Being detached from the illusions of the mind.

Life Force: The conscious energy that flows through all of creation. The vibration of life itself.

Light: The energy and frequency of wisdom, knowledge and the ultimate reality of love. Divine presence.

Love: The only reality. The consciousness of God and fabric of life.

Love of Self: Complete acceptance, embracement and celebration of our Divine essence.

Low-density: The vibrational frequency associated with negativity.

M

Mine: The egos claim to possess.

O

Oneness: The consciousness that embraces the unity of all creation. The full expression of our heightened state of Being.

P

Passion: The swelling of love that surfaces, motivates and consumes a particular objective of desire.

Power: Our innate ability to manifest from intention.

Power of Choice: Our innate ability to manifest from a loving consciousness where the call of our heart becomes the center of intention.

Present moment: The only place where joy, love and celebration can be fulfilled. The perpetual "Now". The ultimate gift to ourselves.

R

Real: The experience of love. What remains the same forever.

Reality: Our perception in relationship to the experience.

Real World: The realm of love consciousness.

S

Sacredness: Considered Holy. Worthy of *spiritual* respect or devotion.

Self Love: Embracing and celebrating all aspects of ones self.

Self Realization: The discovery of one's true nature.

Source Energy: The infinite energy of universal consciousness.

Spirit: The eternal life force that holds consciousness and dwells in the body.

Spirituality: The awareness and embodiment of the laws of the universe.
A deep knowing that comes from within.

Storyteller: The ego-mind, the greatest narrator of illusionary sagas.

Striving: Resistance to the unfolding story. Out of harmony with the flow.

Struggle: Self imposed negativity. Pushing against what is happening.

Surrender: To relinquish the ego's fight into the arms of trust.

T

Transformation: The shifting of our perception away from the Illusion.

Thriving: The exuberant experience of feeling fulfilled.

Trust: The embracement in the divinity and the process of our unfolding story.

Truth: Our Heart-felt wisdom and guidance.

U

Universal Intelligence: The Omnipresent forces that formed our universe.

Universal Law: The commandments that follow the principles of nature.

Universal Truth: What holds real for all of creation.

Unloving: Any thought or action originating from the ego mind. Detached from the heart.

V

Vibrational: The flow of the energy of our life force.

W

Well-Being: The essence of our humanness connected to our quality of life.

Will Power: Our minds dictating and commanding ways to achieving results.

Z

Zero: A number or term that is vibrationally neutral. The absence of perspective or measurement.

Acknowledgments

My deep gratitude to all those majestic beings that crossed my path on this miraculous journey and bestowed to me their gifts of knowledge. My appreciation for the support and love that I received from those who stood beside me as I wandered and stumbled through the maze of my mind-made illusions and the darkness that once clouded my reality. My gratefulness for all the characters who showed up and participated in my theater of life, where the lessons I gleaned from the experiences forever shifted the course I was to follow. I am forever in gratitude for the many spiritual journeys, workshops, authors and healers that presented themselves exactly at the right moment. I am thankful for the constant state of wonderment I experienced as the observer of the synchronicity and divinity of my unfolding story, as I was sacredly shepherded in my spiritual growth. I am honored by the results of the healing experiences that took place amongst my clients and students; and to their constant encouragement for me to share my words and teachings in a book that would be readily available to all. And, of course, the gentle continued guidance and inspiration from Spirit that flowed through me with every word I was led to write. I give my sincere thanks to my dear soul brothers, sisters and comrades, Stephen Koff, Christel Trink, Peter Shane, Jeff Geo, Richie Pollack, Debra Bianco, Cyrus Ontiki, Samuel Kiwasz, Asandra Lamb and Cyndi Curtis who were always there in times of my personal needs, spiritual guidance, encouragement and continued support in my endeavor to bring this book to fruition.

My Heart-Felt Love to the many angels that held my hand and illuminated my path: Cecilia Peres, my greatest spiritual teacher from another star system who guided me over the threshold into a new reality. Brigitte Perreault who recognized my potential to be of service to her subscribers and humanity. Brigitte was responsible for my first introduction to professionally write a monthly article for her global conscious lifestyle publication Perreault Magazine. The beautiful and deeply missed Laura Bella Moire, the "Light" of my life, who gifted me with her divine self, embraced my spirit, supported my intentions and was a reflection of all that I am.

I am eternally grateful to my daughter Tassia Trink and sister Bonnie Pearlman who were my main champions at a time that my health and life were in critical straits. Their devotion, love and selfless support were a healing factor in my recovery which allows us to celebrate this very moment; where we can hold in our hands the profound and reflective wisdoms that I was guided to share on our path to Oneness.

I would especially like to acknowledge two profound and treasured writings that became my pillars and go to bibles over the past years and to this day, as I navigated the valleys and mountains in my exploration of a higher perspective to my life's journey: "A Course in Miracles" scribed through an inner voice to Dr. Helen Schucman and "Oneness" the teachings, received and transcribed by Rasha.

Testimonials

Steven Mana Trink's *Navigating The Winds of Change* takes us on both a personal and a universal journey of spiritual awakening. This fluid and inspired work of prose serenades the reader through the higher wisdom that can only come from someone who has authentically walked their path. Reading the chapters has the effect of a transformation of consciousness. This wonderful book points us in the right direction as well as encouraging us to proceed with love.
~Asandra, Author, Contact Your Spirit Guides,
Schiffer Publishing Ltd.

~~~

Navigating The Winds of Change is a masterpiece of Mana's journey to his awaking and embracement of a new reality. This wonderful book will open the door for the reader to experience his enlightenment and be a roadmap to his own unlimited potential.
~Jeff Gero, Ph.D.

~~~

Steven Mana Trink intimately and prolifically takes you down the path of spiritual transformation and captures the essence of its transcendent healing nature. It is much more than a guide as you are lovingly supported and gracefully nurtured to follow your own path toward loving self - awareness.
~Dr. Stephen Koff DC

~~~

"A beautiful dance through the depths of awareness and the ascent to the embracement of the heart. Bravo….
~Brigitte Perreault, CEO of Ignyte TV

~ ~ ~

"In the beginning, the source of all living beings exists in relationship to each other. In the end, all living beings return to the source. This is "Oneness" and is expertly explained in the wonderful and insightful book by Mana."
~Peter Shane CEO of Herbwell.com

~ ~ ~

I was truly moved by the profound and significant insights and sage observations of a spiritual leader and traveler of God's journey. Navigating The Winds of Change transforms readers as it opens the eye and the heart to pure joy and beauty through inner reflection and release of the ego-centric mind.
~Michael J. Herman, Bestselling author,
columnist and motivational speaker

~ ~ ~

Steven Mana Trink's "Navigating Winds of Change" is Pure Heartfelt Wisdom.
~Randyl Rupar, Founder: Sanctuary of Mana Ke`a Gardens.

For inquiries and comments please contact
stevenmanatrink@gmail.com

You may also visit his website at stevenmanatrink.com

Printed in the United States
by Baker & Taylor Publisher Services